THE CALL OF ISRAEL

OXFORD
UNIVERSITY PRESS
AMEN HOUSE, E.C. 4
London Edinburgh Glasgow
Leipzig New York Toronto
Melbourne Capetown Bombay
Calcutta Madras Shanghai
HUMPHREY MILFORD
PUBLISHER TO THE
UNIVERSITY

THE CALL OF ISRAEL

AN INTRODUCTION TO THE STUDY OF
DIVINE ELECTION

By

W. J. PHYTHIAN-ADAMS

D.S.O., M.C., M.A.

Sometime Scholar of Corpus Christi College, Oxford
Canon of Carlisle
Chaplain to His Majesty the King

WITH 2 MAPS

OXFORD UNIVERSITY PRESS
LONDON: HUMPHREY MILFORD
1934

PRINTED IN GREAT BRITAIN

To

MY FATHER AND MOTHER

IN SURE

AND CERTAIN HOPE

PREFACE

THIS book should be prefaced with a warning. There are still many devoted clergy and laity in the Church of England for whom the critical difficulties of the Old Testament are simply non-existent. In part this is perhaps due to lack of scholarship, in part to lack of interest in the subject: but the dominant cause, without doubt, is a view of the Inspiration of the Holy Scriptures which inclines towards an almost literal inerrancy. If the eyes of any such lovers of the Bible should fall upon these pages, let them be warned that they go forward at their peril: for they will find here a treatment of the written documents which may pain or bewilder them. It is, in fact, the disadvantage of the written word that it is impossible to secure for its audience only those persons whom it may help, not harm; and the author of such a work as this can do no more than salve his conscience by indicating at the outset the type of reader whom his efforts are intended to serve.

Let it be clearly said, then, that this book is meant for those students of the Old Testament who, having struggled with the complexities of critical analysis, have ceased to regard the Hexateuch as providing any reliable information about the early history of Israel. Even here, of course, there will be grades of scepticism, according as the student has or has not advanced from the more conservative views adopted by most English scholars to the radical 'reconstructions' of the narrative favoured most commonly upon the Continent. But the general results of the 'Higher Criticism' must be admitted on the widest view to be the same: it has torn these traditions of Israel into a multitude of heterogeneous fragments and has failed so far to make up any really credible picture out of them. A solution of the existing chaos would seem therefore to be the most urgent need of the moment, and it is this task which claims the major portion of the present work.

Some defence may, perhaps, be necessary for the manner in which this thesis is presented; for it may be charged against the writer that he has indulged his inventive imagination to an extent which must be held improper in the realm of sober scholarship. How far this is true, in particular instances, the reader himself must judge: to the general objection a distinguished pioneer in quite another branch of literature has recently returned an answer which deserves to be quoted:

'No one can understand this (or any other period) without the aid of imagination. . . . One of the curses laid upon modern scholarship is that the scholar must never venture a statement that cannot be supported by a footnote. So the imagination atrophies, and the most learned studies of fact and problem are not only dull in themselves but a cause of dullness in others; for, to say the truth, Learning and Art keep little company together nowadays.'[1]

Beyond recording his profound agreement with this stricture, the present writer has nothing that he can usefully add to it.

Much of the evidence dealing with volcanic and seismic phenomena which is given in the first two chapters of Part III of the present work has appeared in articles in the *Palestine Exploration Fund Quarterly Statement* (July 1930) and in the *Journal of the Palestine Oriental Society*

[1] Dr. G. B. Harrison in *Shakespeare at Work* (Routledge, 1933).

(vol. xii, 1932). The first appendix reproduces, with some alterations and one large addition, an article which appeared in the *Quarterly Statement* under the title 'Israel in the Arabah' (July 1933). The second appendix is reprinted practically verbatim from the *Quarterly Statement* of October 1930.

The Revised Version is followed in all Biblical quotations (Marginal and Septuagint variations being noted where they occur), but the ineffable Name is represented by the conventional transliteration 'Jahweh', in place of the more impersonal 'Lord' or 'God'. The arrangement of poetical passages cited from the prophetic writings is that of Woods and Powell (*The Hebrew Prophets*, Oxford, Clarendon Press, 1909).

The author has much cause to be grateful for the help and counsel he has received, but he desires to make acknowledgement especially to his sister for her patient labour in transcribing an almost illegible manuscript, to his friends Prof. John Garstang and the Rev. A. S. Picton for reading the proofs and offering many useful criticisms and suggestions, and to Miss D. M. Vaughan for her care and interest in compiling the Index and list of Scripture references. That in spite of these many helps the book remains so full of faults and so unworthy of its great subject is a fact of which he is only too conscious and for which he confesses himself alone responsible.

CONTENTS

LIST OF ABBREVIATIONS

Burney, *Judges*.	C. F. Burney, *The Book of Judges*. Rivingtons, 1928.
Driver, *Exodus*.	S. R. Driver, *The Book of Exodus*. (Camb. Bible), 1918.
—— *Notes*.	S. R. Driver, *Notes on the Hebrew Text of the Books of Samuel*. 2nd ed., 1913.
Gressmann, *Mose*.	H. Gressmann, *Mose und seine Zeit*. Göttingen, 1913.
Kittel.	R. Kittel, *Geschichte des Volkes Israel*. 5th and 6th editions, 1923.
Lods, *Israel*.	A. Lods, *Israel from its Beginnings to the Middle of the Eighth Century*. Translated by S. H. Hooke. Kegan Paul, Trench, Trübner & Co., 1932.
LXX.	*The Septuagint*.
Musil, *N.H.*	A. Musil, *The Northern Hejaz*. New York, 1926.
McNeile.	A. H. McNeile, *The Book of Exodus*. (Westminster Com.) 2nd edition, 1917.
Robinson, *History*.	T. H. Robinson, *A History of Israel*, vol. i. Clarendon Press, 1932.
H.D.B.	*Hastings Dictionary of the Bible*.
J.E.A.	*Journal of Egyptian Archaeology*.
J.P.O.S.	*Journal of the Palestine Oriental Society*.
N.C.	*A New Commentary on Holy Scripture*. S.P.C.K., 1928.
P.C.B.	*Peake's Commentary on the Bible*. T. C. and E. C. Jack, 1920.
P.E.F. Ann.	*Palestine Exploration Fund Annual*.
P.E.F.Q.S.	,, ,, ,, *Quarterly Statement*.

WHEN ISRAEL WAS A CHILD THEN
I LOVED HIM AND CALLED MY SON
OUT OF EGYPT.—*Hos*. xi. 1.

INTRODUCTION

IT is required of Christians in these days of chaotic thought that they should show 'how the faith based on the historical revelation of God in Jesus Christ can meet the real needs of the present age, and can apprehend and exhibit the principle of God's reconciling order among human chaos'.[1] Yet it is the dismal truth that too many Christians are themselves in no better case than the world which they are called to redeem. There is, in fact, much 'fear and trembling' in our modern efforts to 'work out our own salvation', but the shuddering awe and self-abasement of which St. Paul was speaking[2] are not so visibly in evidence. Can it be denied that what not only the world but the Church herself in large measure needs to-day is the recovery of that profound conviction of God's overruling Sovereignty, which crowns with an insoluble paradox the mystery of human free-will? *"It is God which worketh in you both to will and to work, for his good pleasure."* Here surely, if we are only willing to seize it, is the clue which can conduct us safely through the labyrinth of our manifold perplexities: for the surrender which this Truth demands of those who will embrace it, is not the abject prostration of will and intellect before a blind World-Force, but the attunement of every faculty to the counsels of an Eternal Love.

It is, in fact, the Christian philosophy of history which is the first and most obvious requirement of this present age: and it must appear strange indeed that Christians

---

[1] O. C. Quick, *The Ground of Faith and the Chaos of Thought* (Nesbit, 1931), p. 112.   [2] Phil. ii. 12.

are so backward in proclaiming it, or even in applying it to the problems of their own lives. For this philosophy lies ready to their hands in the pages of Holy Scripture: it is summed up for them with pregnant brevity in the first chapter of the Epistle to the Ephesians: and they can affirm out of their own experience that whoso drinks of this well of Truth may himself become a fountain of living waters. Nor, again, is this philosophy involved or difficult of comprehension. If a man believes in God, and is not blind to the contagion of evil with which humanity is tainted, he will find in the ordered march of its argument a sublime, straightforward simplicity. Creation, Redemption, the Restitution of All Things—these are the stages by which it measures the progress of the centuries, declaring that apart from them the panorama of earthly history can only be scanned in vain: for these are the turning-points of a Destiny not rooted in human counsels but foreordained by the supreme arbitrament of God. It is God *"who worketh all things after the counsel of his will"*:[1] God, from before all ages calling forth a World into being; God, through a dark background of Sin weaving the golden thread of His Eternal Mercies; God, by His own Arm bringing salvation from the Cross; God, by His Holy Spirit lifting created nature to His Throne; God, Who hereafter shall be even more to His own than Creator, Redeemer, and Sanctifier, but shall be found of them, in a perfect consummation of unity, to be All in all. Here there is more indeed than a mere philosophy of history; there is a 'Gospel of Divine Action'[2] which can set men's souls

---

[1] Eph. i. 11.

[2] Canon Quick has developed this theme in a book bearing this title (Nesbit, 1932).

afire: for out of the heart of this Mystery the Call comes clearly to a Service which is perfect freedom, and the glorious privilege of being fellow workers with God.

That so many among the 'Saints' seem to have lost this Vision cannot be wholly ascribed to the external pressure of their environment. Rather it would appear to be due to a failure of spiritual insight, for which neglect of the Bible must be accounted largely responsible. Neglect, it may be necessary to point out, does not at all imply entire disuse. What is meant here by the term is the habit of concentrating upon particular portions of the Bible with an almost complete indifference to those parts of it which appear less significant or, perhaps, less comprehensible. The results of such a practice can be hardly less disastrous than a refusal to read the Book at all. Not only are those great interpretations of history with which the Epistles abound becoming more and more a *terra incognita* to the majority of English Churchmen, but the entire volume of the Old Testament has now been virtually abandoned, as if the revelation which it contains were too imperfect to be spiritually profitable to Christians.

It may be objected that this last assertion can hardly be substantiated to-day, however true it may have been in the last half-century. That there is, in fact, on all sides a remarkable revival of interest in the Old Testament is undeniable: yet it is gravely open to question whether this interest, as at present directed, will end in a real enlightenment. The position of Old Testament studies in this country is, indeed, so far from being an encouraging one that it can hardly be viewed by a thoughtful Churchman without dismay. It is not merely that the Old Testament (with the exception, perhaps, of certain Psalms and Lessons) is now almost wholly unknown to the majority of Church people; it is much more that many of those who still devote themselves seriously to its contents seem to be treating it with less and less reference to the object which it exists to serve. It is no doubt of considerable interest to the student of Comparative Religion to trace through the writings of the Prophets, the Historians, and the Psalmists the slow development of monotheistic conceptions in Israel. Certainly it is of even greater value to a Christian to note how the idea of God receives with every century an ever-deepening moral and spiritual significance. Yet the Old Testament has been given us, after all, to be something more than a study in religious evolution. First and foremost it claims to be an historical record; a record, moreover, which is unique among the annals of mankind: for it tells how the most High God chose out a Nation for Himself by signs and wonders, and set it apart to be the Servant, and the Temple, of His Glory.

In the face of such a claim two courses would seem open to the Christian student, to test and accept it or to test and reject it: what does not appear open to him, if he has any honest desire for the truth, is to abandon it altogether without even the pretence of a trial. It is hardly an exaggeration to say that we have come perilously near the edge of this moral failure, not so much from a refusal to regard the claim of Israel as credible as from a real indifference to the value of proving it true. Yet a little reflection ought to show us how greatly we need this eventful chapter of history for the support of our faith and the enlargement of our spiritual vision. For Christianity is not only itself an historical religion like Judaism, depending for its sanctions upon a belief

in certain concrete Redemptive Acts of God: it is, in
literal fact, the second chapter of that same Divinely
written Story; the triumphant sequel in which the
tragedy of the Old Covenant is transfigured in the glory
of the New.

Here, then, is the task which awaits us in the following
pages. If we can recover, in however small a degree,
some conception of the reality of those great Events of
the Past, in which the Chosen People discerned, and
responded to, the Call of God, we shall have won for
ourselves at the least a wider prospect of faith, a clearer
view of the methods of that Eternal Craftsman Who
worketh all things after the counsel of His Will. Perhaps,
indeed, we may gain more than this, when we realize
how the leaders of the Old Israel learned from these
same events the more hidden glories of the Mystery of
Election. For we in our turn have known that Call and
that Choosing; we in our turn have inherited its titles
of Love; and it is upon us that has fallen the privilege
and the burden of that Service, which sets us apart as
the Temple of the Indwelling Lord:

> "*But ye are an elect race, a royal priesthood, a holy nation,
> a people for God's own possession, that ye may shew forth the
> excellencies of him who called you out of darkness into his
> marvellous light.*"[1]

[1] 1 Pet. ii. 9, cf. Exod. xix. 5–6.

PART I

THE FAITH OF ISRAEL

Chapter I

THE FAITH OF THE PSALMISTS

TWO 'lying spirits' perpetually haunt the student of the Old Testament. Both are impalpable, and both are for that reason all the more subtly dangerous: and if he does not reckon with them at the outset they will have their way with him.

The first of these is the Demon of Familiarity. Even in these days, when the Bible is perhaps less read and pondered than it was ever wont to be, its story is so well known, as a whole, to the majority of Christians that they are tempted to take the details of it for granted. More especially is this true of those parts of the Old Testament which are recited habitually in congregational worship. Lessons, Psalms, and Canticles have acquired through constant repetition that hard and shining veneer which well-worn objects take on with the passing of the centuries: there is a glaze of familiarity over them which it needs an attentive eye to penetrate. It is here that a malign influence may be detected at work. It is a fact of experience that, in examining what is felt to be already known, we find ourselves strangely reluctant to exert our faculty of attention: we cannot imagine ourselves making any fresh discoveries and we shrink as a result from an effort which seems unprofitable. If this is true of other branches of research, it is peculiarly true of the study of the Bible. It needs a deliberate and sustained exercise of will-power to overcome the delusive sense of familiarity with its contents and to approach them with the freshness of outlook and the underlying thrill of excitement

with which we might land for the first time on an unknown shore.

The second sinister spirit which has to be exorcised
may be called the 'Horror of Miracle'. Of its baleful
effects upon Biblical Criticism it will be necessary to say
more in a later chapter; but a few words by way of
anticipation may not be out of place. Here, once more,
we have to deal with a psychological reluctance to 'think
things out'. A 'miracle' is normally composed of two
parts, the physical phenomenon which is alleged to have
occurred and the supernatural explanation which may
be given of it.[1] Now it is very generally agreed to-day—
among those at least who claim the freedom to judge—
that the particular 'supernatural' explanation which is
assumed for the great Miracles of the Exodus has ceased
to be acceptable to thinking men; and from this it has
been sometimes very rashly concluded that the 'miracles'
themselves never happened at all. But there are obviously two fallacies here. The first is that the destruction of a theory abolishes the fact which it was designed
to explain: the other, that because this particular theory
has failed, a 'supernatural' interpretation must be aban-
doned altogether. Both these inferences are unscientific
and irrational; and it is astonishing that they should have
held the field so long. Yet not only have they held it,
but they have exercised upon Biblical Scholarship an
influence as unhappy as it has been remarkable. To the
former we owe the minimizing rationalizations of so
many of the earlier critics from Wellhausen onwards; to

[1] As, e.g., in the following: "[*The*] *Mount . . . was altogether on smoke,*
BECAUSE *Jahweh descended upon it in fire*" (Exod. xix. 18): or, with the
parts reversed: "*He lifted up the rod, and smote the waters that were in the
river . . .* AND *all the waters that were in the river were turned to blood*" (Exod.
vii. 20–1).

the latter the marked reluctance on the part of some of
our own theologians to lay any stress upon events which
seem too 'supernatural'. The 'Horror of Miracle' has
indeed much to answer for, and there are as yet no
obvious signs that its power has been broken.

When, bearing these cautions in mind, we embark
upon the adventure of discovering afresh the sources of
the Faith of Israel, we can apply the first of them from
the outset by starting with a passage which has become
through our services almost mechanically familiar. Perhaps no better example can be taken than Ps. cxxxvi, with
its well-known refrain: *"For his mercy endureth for ever"*.

This great outburst of thanksgiving opens naturally
with the recognition of the goodness of Jahweh, who is
God of gods, and Lord of lords, and continues (omitting
the refrain) by offering praises

> *"To him who alone doeth great wonders . . .*
> *To him that by understanding made the heavens . . .*
> *To him that spread forth the earth above the waters . . .*
> *To him that made great lights . . .*
> *The sun to rule by day . . .*
> *The moon and stars to rule by night . . ."*

All this is of course the normal language of grateful
devotion, and we should expect it from this point to
follow the general course of another familiar song, the
'Benedicite', in making mention of the other wonders of
God's creative power. But it is now that, if we are alert,
we receive our first shock of surprise. Without any kind
of transitional softening, the Psalmist plunges into the
great events of Israel's Redemption:—

> *"To him that smote Egypt in their first-born . . .*
> *And brought out Israel from among them . . .*

With a strong hand, and with a stretched out arm . . .
To him which divided the Red Sea in sunder . . .
And made Israel to pass through the midst of it . . .
But overthrew Pharaoh and his host in the Red Sea . . .
To him which led his people through the wilderness . . .
To him which smote great kings . . .
And slew famous kings . . .
Sihon king of the Amorites . . .
And Og king of Bashan . . .
And gave their land for an heritage . . .
Even an heritage unto Israel his servant . . ."[1]

There is no parallel to this in the literature of any other
nation, and yet the real and startling significance of it
very often passes undetected. For here is a double paradox. It is not merely that a series of purely historical
events, however memorable and thankworthy, is ranked
without a trace of hesitancy by the side of the great
celestial wonders of the Creation. What is equally, if
not more, extraordinary is that these events themselves,
which are apparently regarded by the Psalmist as solely
deserving of such an honour, are none of them those of
the great days of David or Solomon, but emerge from the
mists of an almost legendary age.

Nor is this particular passage in any way exceptional.
A glance at the other historical psalms reveals the same
emphasis on the same series of happenings. Ps. cxxxv,
for example, another of the 'Songs of Ascents' provides
a very close parallel:

"Whatsoever Jahweh pleased, that hath he done,
*   In heaven and in earth, in the seas and in all deeps.*
*   He causeth the vapours to ascend from the ends of the earth;*

[1] Ps. cxxxvi. 1–9, 10–22.

He maketh the lightnings for the rain;
He bringeth forth the wind out of his treasuries.
Who smote the firstborn of Egypt,
Both of man and beast.
He sent signs and wonders into the midst of thee, O Egypt,
Upon Pharaoh, and upon all his servants.
Who smote many nations,
And slew mighty kings;
Sihon king of the Amorites,
And Og king of Bashan,
And all the kingdoms of Canaan:
And gave their land for an heritage,
An heritage unto Israel his people."[1]

Ps. xcv brings the same two notes into close connexion, a fact which is almost entirely obscured by the Prayer Book translation of the '*Venite*':—

"*O come, let us sing unto Jahweh.*
Let us make a joyful noise to the Rock of our salvation, . . .
For Jahweh is a great God,
And a great King above all gods.
In his hand are the deep places of the earth;
The heights of the mountains are his also.
The sea is his, and he made it;
And his hands formed the dry land.
O come, let us worship and bow down;
Let us kneel before Jahweh our Maker:
For he is our God,
And we are the people of his pasture, and the sheep of his hand.
To-day, Oh that ye would hear his voice!
Harden not your hearts, as at Meribah,
As in the day of Massah in the wilderness:

[1] Ps. cxxxv. 6–12.

When your fathers tempted me,
Proved me, and saw my work . . ."[1]

Here the complete reversal of what we should call the
normal order of faith is both startling and unambiguous.
The devout Jew is not called to worship the Redeemer
of Israel because he is the Maker of all men: he is called
to worship Him as Creator *because* He is Jahweh, the
Rock of Israel's salvation in the wilderness, and because
He then and there made Israel His own peculiar People.[2]
It is the same striking inversion of thought with which
in Ps. cxiv the earth is bidden to tremble at the presence
of Jahweh, not at all because He is the Lord of the
Universe but because He is the God of Jacob before
Whom the mountains skipped, and the sea fled and
Jordan was driven back, in that great Day

"When Israel came out of Egypt".

Nor is it only in the psalms of praise and thanksgiving,[3]
in the shout of jubilation,[4] or in the call to worship, that
we find this unique emphasis on the great events of the
Exodus: it is the same with those in which Israel lifts
up its voice in bitter anguish and despair. In Ps. lxxiv,
the appeal for Divine succour and for vengeance on
those who have destroyed the Temple turns in the first
place to the Power which once wrought so mightily the
deliverance of Israel: only thereafter does it recall what
to us seems naturally paramount, God's sovereign command over all the forces of Nature:

[1] Ps. xcv. 1–9.
[2] The association of the Rock with the water-miracle of Massah-
Meribah (Exod. xvii. 2–7) is, of course, essential to the Psalmist's purpose
(cf. 1 Cor. x. 1–4).
[3] Cf. Ps. lxxxi. 4–10 (The Bondage: Meribah): ciii. 7 (Moses).
[4] Cf. Ps. lxvi. 5–6 (The Red Sea): lxviii. 7–8 (Sinai).

"*Yet God is my King of old,*
Working salvation in the midst of the earth.
Thou didst divide the sea by thy strength:
Thou brakest the heads of the dragons in the waters.
Thou brakest the heads of leviathan in pieces,
Thou gavest him to be meat to the people inhabiting the
wilderness.
Thou didst cleave fountain and flood:
Thou driedst up ever-flowing rivers.
The day is thine, the night also is thine:
Thou hast prepared the light and the sun.
Thou hast set all the borders of the earth:
Thou hast made summer and winter."[1]

The use of poetic imagery has tended here to obscure
the meaning of the allusions; but they would have been
quite clear to any Jewish audience. The dragons (i.e.
the crocodiles which are symbolical of Egypt)[2] are the
pursuing army of Pharaoh (the leviathan), whose bodies,
cast up on the shores of the Red Sea, became food for
the scavengers of the desert, the jackals and hyenas.
The references to the water-miracle of Moses and the
drying up of the Jordan are, of course, explicit.

Perhaps the most striking of all the Psalms in which
this note of remembrance is sounded is that (Ps. lxxvii)
in which the poet relates how he found consolation in his
despondency, when prayer itself had failed to bring him
comfort. It was then, he says, that in the vigils of the
night he pondered the history of the past and faced anew
that terrible and insistent question, *Hath God forgotten to
be gracious? Doth his promise fail for evermore?* Then, with

---

[1] Ps. lxxiv. 12–17.
[2] Cf. Exod. vii. 9 (R.V. Mg.), where the same word is used.

a mighty surge, the conviction of a Love and a Faithfulness which Time cannot alter swept through his heart and flooded it with triumphant joy:

"*Thy way, O God, is in holiness:*
Who is a great God like unto God?
Thou art the God that doest wonders:
Thou hast made known thy strength among the peoples.
Thou hast with thine arm redeemed thy people,
The sons of Jacob and Joseph."

[Selah[1]

"*The waters saw thee, O God;*
The waters saw thee, they were afraid:
The depths also trembled,
The clouds poured out water;
The skies sent out a sound:
Thine arrows also went abroad.
The voice of thy thunder was in the whirlwind;
The lightnings lightened the world:
The earth trembled and shook.
Thy way was in the sea,
And thy paths in the great waters,
And thy footsteps were not known.
Thou leddest thy people like a flock,
By the hand of Moses and Aaron."[2]

This jubilant certitude that God "*hath remembered his covenant for ever, the word which he commanded to a thousand generations*"[3] sounds even louder in Psalms cv and cvi, whether they celebrate His wondrous acts in Egypt and the wilderness or proclaim His mercies in despite of the unfaithfulness of Israel. In the longest of all the historical

[1] Possibly a direction to the orchestra to strike up more loudly (*H.D.B.* s.v.: Kirkpatrick, *Psalms*, p. xxii).
[2] Ps. lxxvii. 13–end (13, R.V. Mg.).   [3] Ps. cv. 8; cf. Ps. cvi. 45.

Psalms (lxxviii) the panorama of this covenanted Love is widened to include the vicissitudes of Israelite history through the disaster of Shiloh up to the establishment of the Temple at Zion. The superficial purpose of this poem is to dwell once more upon the faithfulness of Jahweh and the innumerable trials and provocations to which it was exposed by the sins of Israel. Yet the opening verses seem to disclose a more recondite meaning.[1] The writer is, in effect, discoursing on a deeper mystery, the mystery of Jahweh's Presence in the midst of His People; and his object is to suggest that this Presence has been withdrawn from 'Joseph' (the Northern Kingdom) to dwell from henceforth in the Holy Mountain of Judah. Nor is this quite all; for in closing his meditations at this precise point in history he seems to be marking out for his readers the span of a Sacred Age: the vast perspective of Redemptive Signs and Wonders is to be seen at last as converging upon Israel's Most Holy Place, where, shrouded in thick darkness, the Glory tabernacles behind the Veil.[2]

What impression do we gain from the faith which inspires these Psalmists, most if not all of whom must have lived in post-exilic times? When we realize that a whole millennium at the least separated them from the Events of which they write with so much ardour and conviction, is it not the bare truth to say that such a statement seems almost incredible? Were we to seek some sort of a parallel in our own national history, we should have to conceive of modern Englishmen committing their faith in God and their hopes for the future to a fervent acceptance of the legend of divine assistance

[1] Ps. lxxviii. 1–2.
[2] It is the same thought which inspires the 'priestly' documents of Exodus–Numbers (P.).

C

vouchsafed to King Arthur in his ten ever-glorious victories:

> "*Then Arthur fought against them in those days with the kings of the Britons, and it was he who led their battles . . . The eighth battle was on the castle Guinnion, wherein Arthur bore the image of St. Mary the ever-virgin upon his shoulders, and the pagans were turned to flight . . .*"[1]

The parallel for obvious reasons is inexact, yet it is not altogether idle to make it. A man who in these days was prepared to base his life upon such a memory would be set down without any hesitation as an eccentric. He would be told that those who would gather evidence of God's care for the Nation, must seek it in the pages of recorded history, not in the haze of naïve and superstitious legend. That is precisely what it never seems to have occurred to Israel to do: yet in the issue its Faith, so far from collapsing among the ruins of such frail foundations, has stood as firm as if it were builded upon a rock. However we look at it, there is something here that cries aloud for explanation; something abnormal, something which we might even call a prodigy. For if by that word we mean a phenomenon so portentous and apparently inexplicable that it arouses in the spectator not merely amazement but awe, then this Faith, which has already outlived the latest Psalmist by more than two thousand years, can justifiably claim that title. It is, in truth, a phenomenon in the most literal sense stupendous; and the Events upon which it was grounded seem already to reveal themselves as worthy to be ranked among the few great Wonders of the World.

[1] Nennius, *Historia Britonum*, 9th cent. A.D., quoted by Sir E. K. Chambers, *Arthur of Britain*, 1927, p. 1.

At this point a somewhat obvious objection may be raised. Is there not after all a very simple and ordinary explanation of this inextinguishable Faith of Israel? If it is, in a sense, unique, is not this uniqueness due rather to the impact of the teaching of the prophets than to any very firm belief in the events of so remote a Past? There is an undoubted tendency at the present day to endorse this objection and to accept the alternative which it offers as completely satisfying the conditions of the problem. Two factors have combined to make this view popular. The first, which has already been noticed, is the instinctive revulsion which many modern theologians seem to experience from seeking the source of deeply rooted religious convictions in any historical event of a 'miraculous' character. The other which is at all times its close ally has been aptly described as the 'symbolistic' outlook on history.[1] As opposed to the 'instrumentalist' interpretation of life which sees God as working out His purpose through the ages and intervening actively in the events of human history, the 'symbolistic' view sees the world only 'as a system of signs which manifest God as their meaning'. 'What happens, and the consequence of what happens, becomes much less important. . . . What is needed to realize Heaven indeed is not any catastrophic change in outward reality itself, nor any effort gradually to reform it, but rather a change in the capacity of the soul to see the true inward in and through the outward.'[2]

To such an interpretation of history the teaching of the prophets seems to afford a wholly adequate explanation of the Faith of Israel. From the eighth century B.C.

[1] O. C. Quick, *The Gospel of Divine Action*, 1933, pp. 37, 38.
[2] Ib., p. 387.

down to post-exilic times the Nation received from this great line of spiritual masters an ineradicable grounding in the knowledge of God. His Wrath, His Love, His Righteousness, His Mercy, His unchangeable Faithfulness through the ages to come, all these great Truths were expounded not by one voice only but by a succession of inspired preachers unique in the history of mankind. Here then, surely (it may be urged), is a phenomenon entirely capable of supplying the solution of our problem. Is there really any need to look further or to trouble ourselves with the investigation of a tradition which is at least partially mythical? It may be true that the Events of the great Deliverance were treasured as precious indications of the Love of God for his People. But *even if they never happened at all*, the Faith of Israel would still have survived the storms of the centuries; for the teaching of the prophets would still have remained its chief, if not its only, inspiration.

The value of this argument will be estimated in very different measure by the reader according as he himself belongs to the 'symbolistic' or to the 'instrumentalist' school. If he adheres (with the vast majority of Christians) to the latter, he will at least be well advised to approach it warily. It is, in fact, one of the most pregnant causes of confused thinking at the present day that many of those who accept without hesitation the Hebrew and Christian faith in God's active and continual control of the process of world events, are nevertheless seduced from a whole-hearted allegiance to it by the specious reasonings of the extreme type of symbolist. This is not of course to deny the value, and indeed the necessity, of a 'symbolistic' element in any sane philosophy of religion: the ideal faith is presumably that in which both outlooks are preserved in perfect equilibrium. But what needs to be resisted by the 'instrumentalist' with all his might is the suggestion that because an historical event is a sign which in some degree reveals the character of God, it possesses no intrinsic value of its own as a concrete and outward reality, and that therefore it is really a matter of indifference whether it actually occurred or not. It is precisely this pitfall to which the foregoing 'symbolistic' argument has been softly leading the way; and whatever essential truth it may contain (that it contains much is undeniable), this alone makes necessary a more searching examination of the facts to which it appeals. We shall proceed then, as our next step, to investigate the faith of the prophets themselves, and we shall attempt to discover, if possible, the basis upon which they rested their teaching and the source of that inspiration which played so large a part in moulding and conserving the Faith of Israel.

Chapter II

THE FAITH OF THE PROPHETS

IT will be unnecessary to dwell at length here upon the contributions made by the prophets to the development of the religious consciousness of Israel. The spiritual insight of these great men; their passionate conviction of God's Righteousness, Justice, and gracious Loving-kindness; the fire of their terrible denunciations; the fervour and persuasiveness of their pleading and exhorting voices—all these combine to form so rich a treasure-house of devotion that the Nation for whom they laboured and suffered must have had a heart of stone if it caught no spark from their enthusiasm. And the fact that these voices were not allowed to drift into silence with those of Samuel and Elijah and many another, but echoed imperishably in their writings, to be heard and pondered for all time by their countrymen, secured what had hitherto been unknown in Israel, an undying flame at which the faith of all future generations could be kindled and kept alive. Nor was this all. How great an impetus they gave to the formation of that Sacred Library which we call the Old Testament is even now perhaps not fully realized. They were its mainspring, its creative impulse: their inspiration was the breath which gave it life; which knit together the ancient legends of the Patriarchs, the triumph and solemnity of the Exodus, the struggles of the growing Nation, its glories and its tragedy, into one coherent Form, and revealed Israel to the hearts of its Faithful as the Chosen Servant, the foreordained Ambassador of God.[1]

[1] Isa. xlix. 1–9; lii. 13–liii. 12.

It is, in fact, impossible to exaggerate the extent of the service which the prophets rendered to their country-men. Rather it is a question whether it is not still pro-foundly undervalued. For it is not merely by their approach to a pure Monotheism that their life-work is to be gauged: nor is it only by their insistence upon the moral and spiritual character of the God Whose Oracles they announced: it is much more that, while combining these conceptions, they focused them with a new and fiery intensity upon the inmost soul of the Chosen People of Jahweh. Here again the modern student will need to beware of a prejudice which may blind him to the facts; for it is almost certain that he will normally experi-ence a strong feeling of repulsion when any hint of a Doctrine of Election meets his eye. If he does not over-come this reaction at the outset, he will never grasp clearly and freshly the message which the prophets felt themselves commanded to deliver. For good or ill—and we are not here concerned with passing judgement on them—the prophets were one and all convinced and fer-vent believers in the Call of Israel. It may be said of them, in fact, without the slightest hesitation, that if they had not believed and believed ardently in it, they would never have prophesied at all. They never saw themselves as sent to proclaim a new vision or a new conception of God: they came, as messengers with strict and definite orders, to recall revolting Israel to Jahweh Who had chosen it. This is not to say that in delivering their message they did not in the event go a great deal further. They spoke as the Spirit moved them, and the Spirit moved them mightily. But it is altogether to misunderstand the nature of the service which they rendered to their Nation, if we look for the source of their impulse in any other view of history.

So much it is necessary to say by way of preface; for it is only by freeing our minds from clinging preconceptions that we can recognize the direction in which the teaching of the prophets points, and estimate at its right worth the emphasis which is laid by them upon the great Events of the Past. For them, as for the Psalmists after them, these events are paramount in their significance: they lie at the heart of Israel's faith; of its pride, its love, its gratitude, its inextinguishable hope. Down through the centuries these voices swell and unite into one single heart-stirring cry, *"Remember!"*

The first to utter that cry was AMOS the herdsman of Tekoa (*c.* 760 B.C.), who, almost as he uttered it, knew that it came too late. It is the whole burden of his prophecy that just because Israel had wilfully forgotten the great acts of Jahweh in delivering it from the Egyptian bondage and in providing it with a home from which He had expelled its enemies, it must receive a heavier punishment than any of the surrounding nations whose guilt was the less in that they had not known His mercies:

> *"Yet destroyed I the Amorite before them,*
> *Whose height was like the height of the cedars.*
>
> .   .   .   .
>
> *Also I brought you up out of the land of Egypt,*
> *And led you forty years in the wilderness,*
> *To possess the land of the Amorite.*
>
> *And I raised up of your sons for prophets,*
> *And of your young men for Nazirites.*
>
> IS IT NOT EVEN THUS, O YE CHILDREN OF ISRAEL'?[1]

There is no trace of warning in this voice. Warning

[1] Amos ii. 9-11.

implies some degree at least of innocent ignorance in the guilty, but these had *known* even as they had been known. They had transgressed with their eyes open. They had profaned the Holy Name,[1] acknowledging that it was holy and confessing why for Israel it must always be holy. If their sanctuaries at Bethel and Beersheba recalled to them God's gracious mercies to the Patriarchs, the great High Place at Gilgal aroused an even more exultant memory.[2] It spoke of a day when the waters of Jordan were dried before the feet of Israel and the holocaust of Jericho marked the offering to Jahweh of the first-fruits of the Promised Land. Therefore, there is no uncertainty in the voice which pronounces sentence. It strikes at the heart of men whose own consciences must accuse them:

> "*Hear this word that Jahweh hath spoken against you, O children of Israel, against the whole family which I brought up out of the land of Egypt, saying, You only have I known of all the families of the earth: therefore I will visit upon you all your iniquities.*"[3]

With HOSEA (*c.* 750 B.C.), while the note changes from stern denunciation to tender pleading, the cry itself rings even more loudly than in Amos. Here again it is no new thought which is urged upon Israel, but only an entreaty to remember the Past and be worthy of it. Nor is there any doubt what 'past' it is that Hosea has in mind:

> "*When Israel was a child, then I loved him, And called my son out of Egypt.*"[4]

This is the refrain which runs throughout his prophecies,

---

[1] Amos ii. 7.
[3] Amos iii. 1–2.
[2] Amos iv. 4; v. 4–5.
[4] Hos. xi. 1.

the thought which for Hosea enfolds past, present, and future in one all-satisfying embrace:

> *"I am Jahweh thy God from the land of Egypt;*
> *And thou knowest no God but me,*
> *And beside me there is no saviour.*
> *I [shepherded] thee in the wilderness,*
> *In the land of great drought."*[1]

But Israel had gorged itself with the fat pastures to which He had led it. It had forgotten that it was Jahweh Who had given it the corn and wine and oil. Like an adulterous woman it had taken the Baalim as its lovers and forgotten its only true husband, the Holy One in its midst.[2] What could awake in such an one the memory of past blessings and the love which had been staled by luxury and sensual debauches? To Hosea God's remedy reveals itself as a return to that idyllic life of simple austerity in the wilderness[3] when Israel first appeared to Him in all the charm and freshness of its unspoilt youth:

> *"Therefore, behold, I will allure her,*
> *And bring her into the wilderness,*
> *And speak comfortably unto her.*
> *And I will give her her vineyards from thence,*
> *And the valley of Achor for a door of hope:*
> *And she shall make answer there,*
>   *As in the days of her youth,*
>   *And as in the day when she came up out of the land of Egypt."*[4]

Whether Hosea had some vision of Exile in mind when he wrote this must be regarded as more than doubtful. With Amos he had a simple-living man's horror of 'silken

---

[1] Hos. xiii. 4–5(4, R.V. Mg.). [ ] LXX.
[2] Hos. xiii. 6; ii. 8–13; xi. 9.
[3] Hos. ix. 10.
[4] Hos. ii. 14–15; cf. Joshua vii. 24 f.

cushions' and 'houses of ivory',[1] and he seems to have hoped for a permanent overthrow of what we call 'civilization' and a Feast of Tabernacles indefinitely prolonged:

> *"But I am Jahweh thy God from the land of Egypt;*
> *I will yet again make thee to dwell in tents,*
> *As in the days of the solemn feast."*[2]

Whatever the vision may be which rises here before the eyes of the prophet, it is instructive to notice how his gaze can never stray for long from the great Events of the Exodus. The history of the intervening centuries means little more to him than a tale of sin and misery: it is only in the clean air of the wilderness, where God delivers and Moses leads and preserves the Chosen People,[3] that the spirit of Hosea feels itself at home.

We come now to what is indisputably 'one of the grandest utterances in the Old Testament, and one of the clearest statements of God's demands upon His children'.[4] Though it has found a place among the prophecies of MICAH,[5] it is possible that it belongs to the Northern Kingdom and that its author is yet another of Israel's great Unknown. Here, at any rate, is what has been well described as 'the classical summary of prophetic religion'[6] and here again, with most striking significance, the cry 'Remember!' forms the sole basis of the appeal:

> *"O my people, what have I done unto thee?*
> *And wherein have I wearied thee?*
> *Testify against me.*

---

[1] Amos iii. 12–15. [2] Hos. xii. 9. [3] Hos. xii. 13.
[4] L. Elliott Binns in *N.C.*, p. 588. [5] Micah vi. 1–8.
[6] H. Wheeler Robinson in *P.C.B.*, p. 562.

> *For I brought thee up out of the land of Egypt,*
> *And redeemed thee out of the house of bondage;*
> *And I sent before thee Moses, Aaron, and Miriam.*
> O my people, remember now what Balak king of Moab consulted,
>   *And what Balaam the son of Beor answered him;*
> [*Remember from Shittim unto Gilgal,*][1]
> *That ye may know the righteous acts of Jahweh.*
>
> . . . .
>
> *He hath shewed thee, O man, what is good;*"[2]

In ISAIAH (*c.* 740 B.C.) this emphasis on the Past at
first seems wanting, for there are few explicit references
to the events of the Exodus. Yet the opening words of the
prophet are meaningless, unless this context is supplied:

> "*I have nourished and brought up children,*
>   *And they have rebelled against me.*
>   *The ox knoweth his owner,*
>   *And the ass his master's crib:*
>   *But Israel doth not know,*
>   MY PEOPLE *doth not consider.*"[3]

It is, however, when Isaiah is thinking of Israel's deliverance rather than when he is denouncing their sins that
the memory of the great Redemption slips naturally into
his mind. So in a stirring passage he bids his countrymen
not to be afraid of the Assyrian "*though he smite thee with
the rod, and lift up his staff against thee*", for a mightier than
he has a staff that He will wield again:

> "*As his rod was over the sea,*
>   *So shall he lift it up*
>   *After the manner of Egypt.*"[4]

So again in that yet more glorious Redemption, "*when*

[1] [ ] Prob. a gloss.   [2] Mic. vi. 3–5, 8.
[3] Isa. i. 2–3.   [4] Isa. x. 26 (R.V. Mg.).

Jahweh shall set his hand again the second time to purchase the remnant of his people", He will do a greater miracle even than He wrought through Moses, for *"He will utterly destroy the tongue of the Egyptian Sea"*; and there shall be a highway from Assyria

> *"Like as there was for Israel*
> *In the day that he came up out of the land of Egypt."*[1]

It is to be noticed that in calling upon their countrymen to remember the great acts of Jahweh, the prophets take it for granted that their audience needs no instruction about these. The tradition to which they are appealing is clearly a living one, widely and even deeply rooted in the popular imagination. We may note also that it must have contained much detail which is now lost to us. Hosea's reference to the Valley of Achor is inadequately explained by the events of Joshua vii. 24–6, and the ranking of Miriam by the side of Moses and Aaron (Micah vi. 4) gives her a position for which the present narrative of Exodus and Numbers offers little warrant.[2] It is evident, in fact, that the Israelites of the eighth and seventh centuries possessed a very full tradition of the Nation's Call, and there is no reason to doubt that this had long been in written form. Since the discovery at Ras Shamra of a Canaanite script of the second millennium B.C.[3] we are no longer under the necessity of defending the literacy of early Israel, and the real problem is rather to discover what the original tradition contained. This, however, is a task which must be

---

[1] Isa. xi. 11–16.

[2] Cf. for other examples Ezek. xx. 7–9; Deut. iv. 3–4.

[3] Ras Shamra lies on the Syrian coast between Latakia and Alexandretta. A tablet with a few words in this script is reported to have been found at Beth-Shemash. *P.E.F.Q.S.*, Jan. 1934, p. 2.

THE FAITH OF ISRAEL

deferred till a later chapter:[1] what concerns us here is
the existence of the tradition itself and the new impetus
to ponder and re-examine it which was given by the
prophets from Amos to Isaiah. It was not long before
the interest so fiercely awakened broke into vehement
expression and swept all before it. Out of the dreadful
silence which followed the martyrdoms of Manasseh's
bloody reign the call to remembrance burst forth with
a sudden and terrifying violence; sudden, for it was the
discovery of an hour; terrifying, because it claimed to be
the voice of Moses himself. The problem of the Book of
DEUTERONOMY is still very far from solution, but whatever its origin[2] its effect was instantaneous and permanent.
Not only was it responsible for the drastic religious
reformation set on foot by Josiah, but it moulded for all
time the Jewish conception of the national history. Of
the spiritual grandeur of this book there is no need to
speak here, but it is of the highest importance for our
present purpose to note the basis on which it rested its
appeal. So clear is this, and so often and forcibly repeated, that a single illustration—and that the simplest—
will suffice.

In the twenty-sixth chapter the Israelite is instructed
how to perform his yearly duty of dedicating the first-
fruits of his ground to Jahweh. He is told to put these
in a basket and to carry them to the nearest sanctuary,[3]

[1] See below Part II.
[2] Prof. A. C. Welch's conjecture that Deuteronomy was not connected
with the Josianic reformation, but was a Code of Laws belonging to the
Northern Kingdom, though brilliantly argued in his two books on the
'Code' and the 'Framework', is open to what seem to the present writer
insuperable objections.
[3] Prof. Welch seems to have shown conclusively that the original Code
legislated for a number of Jahweh-sanctuaries and was only amended

where the priest will receive them. Before handing them over the offerer is to say:

"I profess this day unto Jahweh thy God, that I am come unto the land which Jahweh sware unto our fathers for to give us."

The priest is then to take the basket and set it down before the altar (with some appropriate prayer?) after which the offerer is to make a much longer confession of faith:

"An Aramaean ready to perish was my father, and he went down into Egypt, and sojourned there, few in number; and he became there a nation, great, mighty, and populous: and the Egyptians evil entreated us, and afflicted us, and laid upon us hard bondage: and we cried unto Jahweh, the God of our fathers, and Jahweh heard our voice, and saw our affliction, and our toil, and our oppression: and Jahweh brought us forth out of Egypt with a mighty hand, and with an outstretched arm, and with great terribleness, and with signs, and with wonders: and he hath brought us into this place, and hath given us this land, a land flowing with milk and honey. And now, behold, I have brought the first fruits of the ground, which thou, Jahweh, hast given me."[1]

The Bondage in Egypt, the great Redemption, the Covenant at Horeb by which Jahweh bound Israel to Himself, *"to be a peculiar people . . . above all peoples that are upon the face of the earth"*, and finally His gift to them of *"the land which he sware unto their fathers to give it"*, these are the *motifs* which not only animate all the hortatory sermons of Deuteronomy but recur continually in the promulgation of its Code. Great spiritual lessons are drawn at the same time from the phenomena in which

afterwards to meet the needs of Centralization. (*The Code of Deuteronomy*, 1924, pp. 24 ff.)   [1] Deut. xxvi. 3, 5–10.

Jahweh then manifested Himself to His People, but these
are after all incidental to the main purpose of the Book.
That purpose, first and foremost, is not to teach new
truths about the Being and Nature of God but to proclaim unceasingly the great things which He has *done*,
and to proclaim them (once more) not as symbols which
reveal His character, but as outward and visible guaran-
tees of His Choice of Israel and of His power to protect
or to punish it, to bless or to curse. Confronted with the
testimony of these Signs and Wonders, these almost
incredible and yet most substantial proofs of Jahweh's
Love and Sovereignty, what response could be possible
to a faithful Israelite but the offering of a humble and
contrite gratitude and of joyous and unswerving obedience to the Sacred Covenant of his God?

Deuteronomy (or that part of it which was found
by Hilkiah in the Temple) was published in Jerusalem
in the eighteenth year of the reign of King Josiah.[1]
JEREMIAH (according to the statement prefixed to his
book) had begun to prophesy five years before (626 B.C.).[2]
The internal evidence of his earlier chapters confirms
this; for his appeal to the Past strongly resembles that of
Hosea in its portrayal of the unsullied innocence of the
Wilderness years:

> "*Thus saith Jahweh,*
> *I remember concerning thee the kindness of thy youth,*
> *The love of thine espousals;*
> *How thou wentest after me in the wilderness,*
> *In a land that was not sown.*
> *Israel was holiness unto Jahweh,*
> *The firstfruits of his increase . . .*"[3]

[1] 2 Kings xxii. 3.   [2] Jer. i. 2.
[3] Jer. ii. 2 ff. (R.V. Mg.).

Nor is his language coloured by the peculiar phraseology of the Deuteronomist even when he is treating of the same subject:

> "*What unrighteousness have your fathers found in me, that they are gone far from me, and have walked after vanity, and are become vain? Neither said they, Where is Jahweh that brought us up out of the land of Egypt; that led us through the wilderness, through a land of deserts and of pits, through a land of drought and of the shadow of death, through a land that none passed through, and where no man dwelt? And I brought you into a plentiful land, to eat the fruit thereof and the goodness thereof; but when ye entered, ye defiled my land, and made mine heritage an abomination. . . .*
>> *Can a maid forget her ornaments,*
>> *Or a bride her attire?*
>> *Yet my people have forgotten me*
>> *Days without number.*"[1]

Equally significant, perhaps, is the contrast between his abrupt and almost contemptuous allusions to the Ark of the Covenant and to the Temple in which it was enshrined and the later passage, full of echoes of Deuteronomy, in which he calls upon his countrymen to observe and obey this same Covenant.[2] Had the tenth chapter of that book, in particular, been recently published when he wrote his earlier prophecies, it is scarcely conceivable that they would have borne no traces of its influence. In spite, then, of the fact that these two great prophetic voices were raised at almost the same moment, the message of Jeremiah is in no sense derived from the other. From the very first he had insisted, with a passionate conviction, on the faithfulness which might have

---

[1] Jer. ii. 5–8, 32.   [2] Jer. iii. 16; vii. 1–7; xi. 1–8: cf. xxxiv. 13 f.

been expected from the Chosen People of Jahweh, and
he had rested his appeal, like all his predecessors, on the
great Deliverance from Egypt and the gift of the
Promised Land. And even when later he saw no hope
of repentance in his countrymen and no prospect for
them but that of exile, the vision of future restoration
which he contemplated was still coloured by the same
eventful Past:

> *"Behold, the days come, saith Jahweh, that I will make*
> *a new covenant with the house of Israel, and with the house of*
> *Judah; not according to the covenant that I made with their*
> *fathers in the day that I took them by the hand to bring them*
> *out of the land of Egypt; which my covenant they brake . . ."*[1]

No words could reveal more clearly the solid rock upon
which the prophet's faith was founded. However
treacherous and unfaithful Israel proved itself, the bond
which Jahweh had sealed with His own Hand could
never be utterly annulled. The Choice which He had
declared irrevocably by signs and wonders needed no
warrant beyond these facts of History.

Two prophets, respectively of the sixth and fifth centuries, may fittingly bring this brief survey to a close. To
the first of these, EZEKIEL (*c.* 592–570 B.C.), we owe two
of the most remarkable pictures of Israelite history in
the Old Testament. With the earlier passage, the fierce
denunciation of the harlot Jerusalem in chapter xvi, we
are here concerned only in so far as the mention of
Jahweh's 'Covenant' with the hybrid Hittite-Amorite
city of Jebus[2] recalls the establishment in it of the sacred

---

[1] Jer. xxxi. 31–2.
[2] Ezek. xvi. That the 'Covenant' refers to the Theophany at Horeb
is quite impossible, since it is the *Jebusite* city which is being denounced,
not the capital of the House of Judah.

Ark, the visible 'extension' of the Covenant made at the Mount of God and the outward guarantee of Jahweh's Presence. With the later passage we return to the familiar background of the Egyptian bondage, which bears nevertheless traces of an unfamiliar tradition. Practically the whole of the twentieth chapter forms the prophet's reply to certain elders who came to him *"to enquire of Jahweh"*. The answer which they receive is a stern refusal of their request; and this is based on the repeated rebellions of Israel, not merely from the Wilderness days but even from *before* the Deliverance from Egypt. (It will become clear later that there must have been at one time a well-known tradition concerning this earlier period, when Moses returned from the Mount of God and made known the Name of Jahweh to his kinsmen.)[1] Towards the close of his message, however, while still denouncing the transgressions of Israel, Ezekiel changes his strain to one of hope for the future; and here the cast of his thoughts reveals most clearly the school in which they were moulded:

> *"As I live, saith the Lord Jahweh,*
> *Surely with a mighty hand, and with a stretched out arm, and with fury poured out,*
> *Will I be king over you:*
> *And I will bring you out from the peoples,*
> *And will gather you out of the countries wherein ye are scattered, . . .*
> *And I will bring you into the wilderness of the peoples,*
> *And there will I plead with you face to face.*
> *Like as I pleaded with your fathers in the wilderness of the land of Egypt,*

[1] Ezek. xx. 7–9; see below, p. 49 f.

So will I plead with you, . . .
And I will cause you to pass under the rod,
And I will bring you into the bond of the covenant;
And I will purge out from among you the rebels,
  And them that transgress against me;
I will bring them forth out of the land where they sojourn,
But they shall not enter into the land of Israel:

. . . .

And I will be sanctified in you in the sight of the nations.
  And ye shall know that I am Jahweh.
When I shall bring you into the land of Israel,
Into the country which I lifted up mine hand to give unto your
  fathers."[1]

Every step of the ancient Wilderness road is to be trodden again. Once more the uplifted rod;[2] once more the solemnities of the Covenant; once more the gaping of the earth beneath the tents of the gainsayers, the denial of the Land of Promise to the generation of rebels; and for the faithful remnant once more the triumphant entry upon their Divine Inheritance;—such is the vision which represents for Ezekiel the end of the travail of the Chosen People and the dawn of a New Age. And when, in his closing chapters, he reveals the climax of the last great Wandering, it is the Temple that is seen once more as the goal of the pilgrims. Once more the Glory of Jahweh tabernacles amongst them within the Most Holy Place and the Bond of the Covenant of the Mount of God is sealed everlastingly upon "*the mountain of the height of Israel*".[3]

---

[1] Ezek. xx. 33–8, 41–2.
[2] The reference seems to be to the Rod of God, lifted up by Moses over the Red Sea (Exod. xiv. 16).
[3] Ezek. xl–xlviii; xx. 40; cf. above, p. 17 (Ps. lxxviii).

The other voice which may be singled out as illustrating this same appeal to the Past is that of the unknown prophet who has to be called, somewhat cumbrously, TRITO-ISAIAH (*c*. 450 B.C.). But now while the basis of the appeal remains the same, the direction of it is completely altered. It is no longer made to a backsliding Israel with the hope of recalling it to a sense of its privilege and its duty: it is a plea for remembrance which is offered to Jahweh Himself, that He may once again stretch out His Redeeming Hand. Here, then, we approach the point from which we set out. For just as for the 'priestly' editors of the Pentateuch the great Temple-vision of Ezekiel created at once a pattern and an ideal, so for the post-exilic psalmists this passionate cry for succour awakened echoes never thereafter to be silenced. While the beauty and tenderness of the whole passage make it difficult to resist the temptation of quoting it at length, we must content ourselves with the opening stanza:[1]

> "*I will make mention of the lovingkindnesses of Jahweh, and the praises of Jahweh, according to all that Jahweh hath bestowed on us; and the great goodness toward the house of Israel, which he hath bestowed on them according to his mercies, and according to the multitude of his lovingkindnesses. For he said,*
> *Surely, they are my people,*
> *Children that will not deal falsely:*
> *So he was their saviour.*
> *In all their affliction he was afflicted,*
> *And the angel of his presence saved them:*[2]

[1] Isa. lxiii. 7–14.

[2] Or with LXX. 'No messenger or angel, but His own Presence saved them.' Cf. Exod. xxxiii. 14.

In his love and in his pity he redeemed them;
And he bare them, and carried them
   All the days of old.
But they rebelled, and grieved his holy spirit:
Therefore he was turned to be their enemy,
And himself fought against them.

   Then his people remembered the ancient days of Moses,[1]
Saying, where is he that brought up out of the sea the shep-
   herd of his flock?[2]
Where is he that put his holy spirit in the midst of them?[3]
That caused his glorious arm to go at the right hand of
   Moses?[4]
That divided the water before them, to make himself an
   everlasting name?
That led them through the depths, as an horse in the
   wilderness,
   That they stumbled not?
As the cattle that go down into the valley,
The spirit of Jahweh caused them to rest:[5]
So didst thou lead thy people,
   To make thyself a glorious name."

So when the rebellious Nation has expiated its guilt
in exile and dispersion it is the thought of the same
mighty acts and mercies of Jahweh which keeps alive its
hopes and inspires its visions; and it is the same faith which
persists unconquered through the centuries. It is perhaps
not wholly by accident that the last words of the Old
Testament echo this age-long cry:

[1] R.V. Mg.
[2] i.e. Moses. The reading is that of some versions and MSS.
[3] Num. xi. 17; 25–9. (The Seventy Elders.)
[4] i.e. the Rod of God in Moses' hand. (Exod. iv. 20; vii. 17; xiv. 16.)
[5] Cf. Exod. xxxiii. 14; Num. x. 33. The reference is to the 'resting-places' chosen for Israel by Jahweh's Presence (Panim) in the Ark.

"Remember ye the law of Moses my servant, which I com-
manded unto him in Horeb for all Israel, even statutes and
judgements.

Behold, I will send you Elijah the prophet
Before the great and terrible day of Jahweh come.
And he shall turn the heart of the fathers to the children,
And the heart of the children to their fathers;
Lest I come and smite the earth with a curse."[1]

[1] Mal. iv. 4–6.

Chapter III

THE FAITH OF THE FATHERS

OUR rapid survey of the great line of prophetic messengers will have sufficed, it is hoped, to make two points clear. First, it is impossible to dissociate their moral and theological teaching from their fervent faith in the great Redemptive Acts of Jahweh from the borders of Egypt to the settlement in the Land of Promise. Their religion is nothing if it is not from first to last historical. They are driven to speak solely because of what they believe has been done for Israel in the remote Past. Nor does their interpretation of that Past vary, however much they may differ from one another in spiritual perception or mental outlook. The God whose hands wrought these signs and wonders may be for one a God of wrath, for another a God of love: for one He may be a God Who rejects all offerings but those of righteousness and obedience; for another He may be a God Who demands a Temple, a Priesthood, an elaborate ritual, and an ordered system of sacrifices. Yet in one thought all are united. They have no doubt what Jahweh meant by His actions: *He declared by them to the world that He had chosen Israel*. That was radical. Everything else must spring, must be deduced, from that. And if for any reason the memory of the great events which guaranteed this Election were ever permitted to disappear, Israel as a Nation or even as a religious community must inevitably vanish with it.

The second point is one to which we have already alluded, but it is of such importance that it cannot be too strongly emphasized. If it is true that the faith of post-exilic Israel was kindled and kept alive by the study of the great prophetic writers from the eighth century onwards, it still remains to ask whence these writers themselves derived their convictions and how they were able to assume a knowledge of the main facts in their contemporaries. The problem, in other words, so far from being solved, is merely shifted backwards into a still earlier age; and it becomes correspondingly clearer where the true answer lies. It becomes necessary, in short, to assume the existence of a strong and living Tradition faithfully preserved through the centuries and constantly expounded by the religious teachers of the Nation. Such a Tradition must in any case have come into being with the recovery of the Sacred Ark by David and the erection of its gorgeous sanctuary by Solomon. But here, too, it is impossible to call a halt. It is necessary to go back still farther to that earlier sanctuary of Shiloh with its yet more ancient priesthood, and to ask ourselves what traditions must have been preserved *there* from the earliest times. Nor again is this all. When we read what is one of the oldest documents in the Old Testament, the Song of Deborah, we cannot fail to be struck by the astonishing fervour with which the prophetess denounces the absent tribes, and the fury with which she curses the unknown Meroz because it had not helped Jahweh against the mighty. Yet the real significance of this poem is even now too often overlooked.[1] Not only does it refute the theory that the tribes arrived in Canaan at different epochs, from opposite directions and with various origins,[2]

---

[1] It is, however, given full weight by Lods (*Israel*, p. 309 f.).

[2] This theory was advocated strongly by the late Prof. C. F. Burney in *Israel's Settlement in Canaan*, Schweich Lectures, 1917.

but it proves (by its very assumption that even the most distant must rally to the Divine Summons) that the Nation was already serving Jahweh as a united whole before it even entered the Land of Promise. Although the reference to Sinai is an obvious interpolation which breaks the rhythm,[1] the description of Jahweh's advance over 'the field of Edom' may well be part of the original poem. If this is so the evidence is still more cogent, for it points beyond Mt. Seir to some centre of unity further south. It is in fact the Faith of Israel itself which is seen here advancing upon Canaan from the Wilderness.

Again and again, then, the question returns upon the reader and refuses to be burked: *What brought that Faith originally into being?* It must be replied that three factors at least must have been present: the bare events in themselves, the intellectual genius which could invest them with supernatural significance, and the ability and willingness of the people at large to accept this significance as compellingly, unquestionably true. On the middle of these three terms it is perhaps unnecessary to dwell at length; for it is filled with entire adequacy by the figure of Moses. When a great name is handed down through the centuries, and especially when it is surrounded with every tribute which awe and reverence can offer, it may be reasonably surmised that the man who bore it possessed a real eminence in those things for which he is praised. The traditional glory of Moses is not that he was a warrior or a philosopher, nor even that he was the founder of a new religion, but that he was a servant sent by Jahweh to bring His People out of Egypt, to instruct them in the rules which must govern their new

[1] Burney, *Judges*, p. 109. The name Sinai is probably a post-exilic insertion. See below, p. 131.

national life, and to launch them thus equipped upon
the Promised Land. The man who in leaving such a
memory of his life-work succeeded so amazingly in trans-
ferring the greater glory to his God must have been
endowed with a moral stature little, if at all, short of
that which is ascribed to him. Nor is there any *a priori*
impossibility in this. The view which regards such religious genius as inherently impossible in the middle
of the fifteenth century B.C.[1] is not merely prejudiced:
it overlooks the fact that hardly half a century later
an almost monotheistic Faith was being proclaimed in
Egypt in hymns which are comparable with the noblest
Psalms of Israel.[2] There are, in fact, no rational objections to the traditional estimate of the spiritual eminence
of Moses, while there are abundant reasons for accepting
it. That a mass of sacred legend has been attached to
his name is a fact which must be obvious to any candid
student of the documents: that the man himself was less
than the greatest of religious leaders is an unproved
assumption, which effects nothing save to render the
problem insoluble.

What, then, of his people? Here a great deal depends
upon the view which is taken of the traditions of the
patriarchal age; and it is necessary to ask how far they
may be regarded as reliable. The Bene Israel claimed
to be descended from Abraham the Hebrew, who
migrated from his homeland in Northern Mesopotamia
(Harran) and became a notable sheikh in southern
Canaan. If the reference to Ur of the Chaldees in Gen.

---

[1] Cf. Gressmann, *Mose*, p. 443: "*Zweitens widerspricht sie dem Geist der Antike.*" If a later date for the Exodus is assumed, the evidence is pro-
portionately stronger.

[2] Breasted, *History of Egypt*, 2nd ed., p. 371 f. (Ps. civ).

xi. 29–31 is really to be read Arphaxad as has been suggested by some scholars,[1] the original home of the patriarch must be placed still farther to the north, most probably in the mountains of Armenia, as the legend of the Ark's resting on Ararat suggests. (The Armenoid characteristics of the most enduring Jewish type seem to offer a further corroboration of this view.) However this may be, the presence of the patriarchal names Terah, Nahor, and Serug in the region of Harran[2] so far confirms the tradition of Genesis, and endorses the statement of the Deuteronomist quoted above: "*An Aramaean . . . was my father.*"

While the consciousness of this remote northern origin was kept alive in Israel, the later migration to Palestine might be expected to leave a memory not less clear. That it did so, even to some matters of specific detail, is evident from the fragments of the ancient tradition which are all that survive to us in the Book of Genesis. These details, it should be noted, are not merely connected with the religious practices of the Patriarchs: they are concerned equally with their personal and secular affairs. At Hebron, Abraham purchases a field and cave for a family burying-place: at Shechem Jacob buys a 'parcel of ground' for his tent (or wins a 'portion' from the Amorite with his sword and bow): at Beersheba it is not a religious issue which is involved between Abraham (or Isaac) and Abimelech, but the purely material consideration of who shall possess the wells.[3]

It is of course objected to the credibility of these stories

[1] Cf. Albright, *The Archaeology of Palestine and the Bible*, Revell, 1932, pp. 139, 209–10. Arphaxad is probably the later Arrapachitis on the S. border of Armenia, with its capital at Arrapkha (modern Kirkuk).

[2] Ib., p. 139.

[3] Gen. xxiii; xxxiii. 19 (xlviii. 22); xxi. 22–32 (xxvi. 17–33).

that they are much more probably the product of a later age, and that so far from being genuine memories, they have been invented to give the sanction of venerated names to what were in reality the high-places of Canaanite divinities. This is certainly a possibility, but it cannot be regarded as more; and it should be noted that there are several facts which remain inexplicable if these stories are to be treated as wholly fictitious. There is, for example, the curious absence in the Book of Judges of any tradition about the capture of the central highlands around Shechem. That this territory was not only occupied by Israel at an early date, but formed the heart of its defences, is evident from the selection of Shiloh (*Seilun*) as the most suitable location for the Sacred Ark. This certainly suggests that the patriarchal legend contains a substratum of truth. Another curious and unexplained feature of the later years is the popularity of Beersheba with the *Northern* Kingdom.[1] There must surely have been an unusually strong incentive to worship at this place when the great sanctuaries of Bethel, Gilgal, and Dan were so much more accessible. We might note also as significant the solemn conveyance of Jacob's body to Hebron and the removal of the bones of Joseph from Egypt and their subsequent interment in 'the parcel of ground' at Shechem. There seems no special point in either of these traditions unless it is that they narrate what actually occurred.

Considerations such as these are by no means few in number or negligible,[2] and they all seem to corroborate

---

[1] Amos v. 5; viii. 14.

[2] Note also small topographical details like the tomb of Rachel (Gen. xxxv. 20: 1 Sam. x. 2), and the stone of Bohan son of Reuben (Joshua xv. 6; xviii. 17).

what we are told in Genesis of the movements of the Patriarchs. Through a cloud of folk-lore, many details of which are certainly not to be trusted, there emerges none the less a picture of that age, inherently probable and not to be analysed away. That the Patriarchs themselves were historic personages and not merely tribal symbols is a view widely held to-day which marks the return of a soberer method of criticism.[1] There is, however, one argument in its favour which it may perhaps be useful to stress here. The most remarkable feature of the surviving tradition is to be found not in the predominance of Abraham and Jacob, but in the insignificance of Isaac. The space which is devoted to him in Genesis can hardly be said to belong to him at all, for the opening chapter of his life is included in the last years of Abraham, and the closing in the first years of Jacob;[2] and even when Isaac is left to act by himself, the stories told of him are obvious duplicates of the adventures of his father.[3] There appears, in fact, to be nothing of importance about this patriarch except that he actually lived and begat a more famous son. As a tribal symbol he has no 'survival-value': as a father and a link with the past he becomes an honoured memory.[4]

There remains finally one question on which a word must be said. It concerns the actual constitution of the Bene Israel in Egypt. When the prevailing view of the Exodus was that it took place in the reign of Merneptah (c. 1225 B.C.), the discovery of the name of Israel on the stela of this monarch, and of that of Asher in the Pales-

---

[1] So Albright argues for the historicity of Joseph (op. cit., p. 149 f.); cf. Robinson (*History*, p. 54) and Lods more tentatively (*Israel*, p. 158).   [2] Gen. xxiv and xxvii.

[3] Gen. xxvi. 1–12, 17–33; Gen. xx. 1–18; xxi. 22–34.

[4] Cf. Amos vii. 9, 16.

tinian records of his predecessor Ramses II, made it at least plausible to conjecture that it was not the whole of the historic Twelve Tribes that took refuge in Egypt.[1] To-day, however, it is becoming more and more probable that the premiss of this argument is incorrect, and that the Exodus took place in the reign of Amenhotep II (c. 1440 B.C.).[2] There is therefore no longer any *a priori* reason for distrusting the tradition of Genesis on this point (it is very strongly corroborated, as we have seen, by the Song of Deborah), and we may take it as a working hypothesis that the people to whom Moses brought his message of deliverance represented the twelve historic tribes of the future Nation of Israel.[3]

An attempt may now be made to determine the third of those factors which must have been present when the Faith of Israel was born: namely, how far the people themselves were capable of comprehending, and responding to, the call of Moses. We are entitled to assume, in the first place, in the mass of them a definite awareness of their ancestral past and at least some vague remembrance of the God of the Patriarchs. The religion which their forefathers had brought to Egypt in the days of Joseph must have been, at the lowest, the El worship of a semi-nomadic race: at the highest it may have been something much more advanced.[4] It has been noted that

[1] So Burney, *Schweich Lectures*, 1917, and *Judges* (Introd. § 6).

[2] So T. E. Peet (*Egypt and the O.T.*, 1922); J. W. Jack (*Date of the Exodus*, 1925); Garstang (*Joshua, Judges*, 1931). The evidence discovered by Garstang at Jericho seems to be conclusive for the earlier date. (See *Annals of Arch., Liverpool*, xx, pp. 22, 42.)

[3] It should be remembered also that many *Hebrews* may have remained in Palestine who were not *Israelites* (cf. 1 Sam. xiii. 3; xiv. 11, 21). The relations of the Khabiru of the Amarna Letters to the Israelites is still undetermined. (See Albright, p. 132; Robinson, p. 76 f.)

[4] Gen. xxxv. 1–8 (one of the older sources) relates an abjuration of

'in the religions of the tribes and of the clans the divine being [EL] was gradually ceasing to be the vague spirit of a spring or a mountain, and becoming more and more the chief of a human group, the god of the "fathers" of this group, and hence a *person*. This is apparently the force of the word *'el* in the various names of the tribes and peoples with which it is compounded: *Ishmael*, the god (of the tribe) hears; *Jerahmael*, the god is merciful; *Israel*, the god strives; *Jacobel*, the god is cunning.'[1] Further, it is a remarkable fact that until the introduction of the divine Name Jahweh, this 'god of the fathers' seems to have remained a remote and vague conception if not entirely an impersonal one. There is at any rate no known example of a pre-Mosaic Hebrew name in which the particular El of the group (tribe or clan) is specially denoted.[2] It would therefore be perfectly natural for Moses to appear before his countrymen as a messenger from the El of their great ancestors and to claim His authority and promise His assistance by disclosing with all solemnity His secret Name and thus revealing Him not merely as a Power but as a Person. Such a step was in any case inevitable if he was to accomplish his mission; for no nameless spirit could be trusted to succeed in delivering his people, when there were ranged against him all the vast mysterious forces which pulsed behind the great names of the Egyptian pantheon. From the outset it was to be a battle royal, in which the Divine Champion of Israel must take the field without disguise:

"*Thus saith Jahweh, the God of the Hebrews,*
Let my people go, that they may serve ME."[3]

'strange gods' undertaken at the bidding of Jacob on his return to Canaan.

[1] Lods, p. 252.   [2] Ib.   [3] Exod. ix. 1.

Before this could be, however, a serious obstacle had almost certainly to be faced. It is sometimes taken for granted that the Israelites retained their ancestral worship after their migration to Egypt and that they needed only the revelation of the Name of Jahweh to arouse their hopes and prepare them for the escape from bondage. But this must be regarded as at the least improbable. If in later years Jahwism itself, with all the accumulated efforts of the prophets to enforce it, failed altogether to shatter the hold which the Queen of Heaven had gained upon the popular imagination,[1] the vague El worship of the semi-nomads of the Negeb must have had little chance of surviving transplantation to the Delta. It is true that according to one tradition the Bene Israel were segregated in the land of Goshen from the main currents of the Nile life, but even if this memory is primitive and authentic, these favourable conditions must have been greatly modified, if not entirely cancelled, when the great building schemes of the Pharaoh brought the Hebrews into immediate contact with their masters. Two forces in any event must have worked continually to submerge their old religious conceptions; the glamour of an ancient civilization which had been led by Amon Re' to the conquest of an Empire, and the dominant and universal belief in all the settled countries of that epoch that the gods of a particular region were the gods to be propitiated and obeyed. It has been noticed above that some trace of what may well be a genuine tradition of this Egyptian influence finds expression in the writings of Ezekiel:[2]

"In the day when I chose Israel, and lifted up mine hand unto the seed of the house of Jacob, and made myself known unto them in the land of Egypt, . . . I said unto them,

[1] Jer. xliv. 15–19.   [2] Ezek. xx. 5–8.

E

> *Cast ye away every man the abominations of his eyes,*
> *And defile not yourselves with the idols of Egypt: I am*
>   *Jahweh your God.*
> *But they rebelled against me,*
> *And would not hearken unto me;*
> *They did not every man cast away the abominations of their*
>   *eyes,*
> *Neither did they forsake the idols of Egypt:*
> *Then I said I would pour out my fury upon them,*
> *To accomplish my anger against them*
>   *In the midst of the land of Egypt.*"

In the earliest of the surviving documents of Exodus no explicit reference to this tradition is now to be found.[1] It would appear indeed that it was only in a later day, when the prophets were driven to emphasizing the past unfaithfulness of Israel, that these more painful episodes were exposed and dwelt upon. Yet even so, while there is no direct allusion in Exodus, there seems to be at least a hint of this uneasy memory. It is to be found in the doubt of his own people's loyalty which Moses utters almost immediately after his call:

> "*Behold they will not believe me, nor hearken unto my voice.*"[2]

At this point in the narrative there begin two parallel lines of tradition in which the 'signs' to be wrought by Moses have entirely different objects.[3] In the one they are intended exclusively to convince the Israelites; in the other they are demonstrations of Jahweh's power, which

---

[1] It is possible, however, that traces of the original tradition are to be found in the fragment Exod. vi. 10–13, where the refusal of Israel to hear Moses is represented as a *later* phase brought about by the increased agony of the Oppression.

[2] Exod. iv. 1.　　　　　　　　　　　[3] Exod. iv. 1–9, 21–3.

are directed solely against the stubbornness of the Pharaoh. It is, of course, the first of these with which we are dealing here. In the sequel as it now stands we are merely told that (not Moses but) Aaron did the signs in the sight of the people, and that the people believed and worshipped. Two considerations make it almost impossible to accept this as the original conclusion of the story. In the first place the prominence of Aaron as the agent and representative of Moses is one of the most easily recognizable characteristics of the latest and least trustworthy redaction. But an equally grave objection is that the signs themselves are 'wasted'. No good story-teller would ever be content with this lame and abbreviated conclusion, which, after the reader has been prepared for a gradual winning over of the people, betrays his awakened interest by making the success immediate. It is hardly disputable that the original narrative told a very different story and one much more nearly akin to the situation which Moses must actually have faced. His first task must have awaited him long before he challenged the Pharaoh: it was to convince and to convert his own kinsmen.[1]

All the main elements of the problem but one have now been passed in review, and it should be possible to arrive at a provisional estimate of the factor which still remains unknown, namely, the character of those events which created the Nation, and determined the Faith, of Israel. It is important in the first place to realize the magnitude of the achievement which was accomplished through the genius of Moses by their means; for it is an apparently unbridgeable gulf which separates the sojourn in Egypt

---

[1] The significance in this connexion of the curious statement in 1 Sam. ii. 27–8 (Elidae) is discussed below, p. 86.

from the settlement in the Land of Promise.[1] On the one side of this gulf there is to be seen a heterogeneous population of Hebrews, a small nucleus of whom form the clans of the Bene Israel, while the large majority are of mixed and unknown origin. Admitted some generations previously to the rich pasturages of the Delta and all the other material benefits of a highly developed civilization, these semi-nomad migrants from an austere and primitive environment have long since lost the simplicity of their ancestral stock. They have succumbed with equal pliability to the faiths and the flesh-pots of their new home; and neither the memory of the past nor the conditions of the present have hitherto supplied a motive for abandoning either. But now out of a blue sky has come disaster. The Pharaohs who befriended these sojourners have been swept out of the country, and their Delta capital has been turned into a base for the military expeditions of their conquerors. For this new Dynasty has developed a boundless ambition for empire, and an equally insatiable demand for human labour. From a peaceful solitude the western frontier of the Delta has become a highway for the Egyptian armies, marching or sailing away each year on their Syrian campaigns and each year returning laden with spoil and clamouring for new equipment. Arsenals, stores, workshops, granaries spring up on all sides to supply their needs; and since none of these can be constructed without man-power, the wretched Hebrews are speedily condemned to the

[1] In the picture which follows, the 'Oppression' is ascribed to Thothmes III, the greatest Pharaoh of the (XVIIIth) Dynasty which expelled the Hyksos. The Pharaoh of the Exodus is his successor Amenhotep II (1448–1420). The Hyksos capital Avaris became later the 'Delta capital of the Ramessides' and later still the city of Tanis (Zoan). (A. J. Gardiner, *J.E.A.*, vol. xix, pp. 122–8.)

corvée. Meanwhile all hope of escape has been extinguished, for the frontier-wall of the Syrian desert has
been garrisoned from sea to sea.[1] Hemmed in on all sides,
and utterly at the mercy of their masters, they can look
for no future but one of abject serfdom.

On the other side of the gulf, these same Hebrews
emerge from the wilderness no longer an inchoate multitude of slaves but a compact self-conscious Nation,
fighting with ruthless ferocity the 'Wars of Jahweh'.[2]
With surprising discipline and mobility they fling themselves at the formidable armies which are mustered to
oppose them and by two smashing blows annihilate all
organized resistance. The strongly walled cities continue
to defy them, but they settle nevertheless unchallenged
in the conquered territory; and, even when thus dis-
persed, one Code of Laws governs them, one memory of
the Past inspires them, one Covenant unites them, and
one Sacred Name claims their indefeasible allegiance.

It would obviously be easy to extend and heighten
this contrast, but it would be superfluous. Indeed it would
have been unnecessary to say even so much, were it not
that the whole of this story is at once too familiar and too
'miraculous'. Here, perhaps more than anywhere else
in the study of the Old Testament, we have to reckon with
these two deluding influences. There is the danger on

---

[1] This is admittedly an inference, but it is based (*a*) on the fact that
the wall existed (Breasted, *History of Egypt*, 2nd ed., 1920, p. 447); and
(*b*) on the obvious conclusion that if it had not been guarded, the
Israelites would have escaped through or over it, and not through the
Sea. The Gulf of Suez seems to have included the Bitter Lakes at this
period: even in the first half of the nineteenth century A.D. strong tides
could still cover the low-lying stretches between these lakes and the sea.
(Mallon, *Orientalia*, 1924, p. 158.)

[2] Num. xxi. 14. For a study of Joshua's tactics see Garstang, *Joshua,
Judges*. 1931, pp. 153 ff.

the one hand of sliding over the surface of the facts as presenting no need for explanation, because they are in some vague sense 'Biblical'; while on the other there is the temptation to pass by them with averted eyes, from an uneasy suspicion that they must be wholly fabulous. Once these two fatal seductions have been rendered powerless and the problem is grasped with a vigorous and resolute attention, it is impossible any longer to resist the one palpable conclusion that, in some sense at least, the change must have been worked by a miracle. Indeed the case can be put much more strongly; for it is extremely doubtful whether a single miracle could have sufficed to produce such an effect, however highly we rate the strength of the personality of Moses. On this point, however, we have no need to speculate. The records which represent for us the immemorial Tradition of Israel lie open for our examination, and the testimony which they have to offer will be found not only striking but decisive.

PART II

THE TRADITION

Chapter I

THE STRUCTURE OF THE TRADITION

*T*HE *Tradition which we are to investigate is an immaterial*
Reality, not an historical treatise: it is the living Memory
which inspired the Faith of Israel, not that shadow of it which
survives in the Books of Exodus and Numbers.

It is all-important to grasp this firmly from the first,
for centuries of misunderstanding have almost succeeded
in blinding us to the truth. It might indeed have been
thought that when the value of Biblical Criticism had
once been firmly established, the significance of its
epoch-making discoveries would have been speedily and
fully realized. Yet its scientific and decisive disentangle-
ment of the main documentary strata of these books,[1]
which is now so much of a commonplace in the world
of scholarship, still fails as a whole to effect that complete
re-orientation of thought which is the only logical outcome of such a revolution.

What position are these documents now to hold in our
estimation? What relation are we to think of them as
bearing to the Tradition of which they form a reflection
now admitted to be imperfect? These are questions
which it would seem natural to treat as primary; and yet
it is a matter for speculation whether they are being asked
at all. The general attitude of modern Biblical Scholar-

[1] The sources are distinguished as the Jahwist or Judean (J); the
Elohist or Ephraimite (E); a redaction inspired by Deuteronomy or
from the same prophetic school (Rd); the Priestly (P) which is largely,
if not entirely, post-exilic; and a redaction made by priestly writers
(Rp). These broad distinctions are accepted throughout the present
work, and subdivisions of them, which are more disputable, can be
ignored.

ship seems rather to be that of an exhausted conqueror who is unable or unwilling to exploit his victory to the full. The gains are there, if he will reap them by a vigorous initiative; but he prefers to consolidate his advantages upon the ground which he has won.

This policy of inertia, which has seldom proved successful in other spheres, is in this case unusually damaging to the cause which it seeks to serve; for it has halted at the exact moment when it should have advanced with ruthless ardour, and the compromise which it has accepted is, in effect, no compromise at all. The cause of this disaster is a very simple one. It had been hoped that when critical analysis had separated out from the medley of documents those sources which might be treated as the oldest and therefore the most reliable, the task of the historian of ancient Israel must become comparatively straightforward. But this is a fond delusion. Whatever it was that really happened "*when Israel came out of Egypt*", it will not be discovered by treating these heterogeneous fragments as the component parts of a puzzle-picture, which can be 'reconstructed' provided the right pieces are used. Nor, again, is the truth to be extracted by more and more complex surgical operations upon J or E, or upon any of their now rapidly increasing progeny. In *that* sense, we can never hope to hold it in our hands at all. If we find it, it will rather be by observation at long range; by a broad panoramic survey such as that which must be made by an archaeological explorer who is forced to examine his objective from the air. Indeed it may not be unprofitable to dwell upon this comparison, for it will at least emphasize what is the principal and inherent difficulty of the whole undertaking.

We must attempt, then, to view the tradition, as we should be driven to inspect a huge forsaken ruin, buried in the heart of an impenetrable wild. We can never get close enough to such a building to be able to clear and measure and examine it with our own hands: we can only fly low above it and around it and beside it, and make our observations of its visible structure as we pass. We notice then that it very strangely resembles the famous Wailing Wall at Jerusalem, in that it is largely made up of a mosaic of separate stones, wrought and rewrought through many ages and through many hands. There, near ground level, we can see the enormous blocks which seem to speak of the spacious days of a nation in its glory; and, above them, course by course, an astonishing patchwork of masonry, much of it very obviously made up of older materials reshaped and re-used by generations of pious builders. But below? Are there here, too, as at Jerusalem, those seventy invisible feet of immemorial foundations, resting immovably on the rock of the Mount of God? There we touch at last the heart of our problem. For it is these about which we must somehow discover the truth; these, not the upper courses, which only seem to indicate their presence and may or may not disclose the plan to which they conform.

This is our problem, as it may not unfairly be stated; and now two features at least are becoming abundantly clear. First, it must be obvious that whatever evidence we may be able to gather must, in the nature of things, be what is called 'circumstantial'. We can never hope for strictly scientific certainty. This means, of course, that our conclusions can only be of the broadest description: there will be no one detail of which we shall be able to say, 'This was so': for we shall have abandoned the hopeless task of identifying the work of later ages with the primal base which is buried for ever from our eyes. If, in consequence, our results appear somewhat disappointingly meagre, we shall be wise to estimate them not by their size but by their strength; and to content ourselves with evidence which is at least not less convincing than that which is thought valid in England when a human life is at stake.

Secondly, as to the means at our disposal: and here our simile is particularly helpful and suggestive. As the archaeologist is enabled by his expert knowledge not merely to distinguish the difference of age between separate courses of the structure but to detect, by the idiosyncrasies of their dressing and tooling, the intrusive presence of individual stones, so we, through the labours of generations of critical scholars, can discriminate in the texture of the documents not only the larger divisions of datable material but even the isolated and independent interpolations. The value of this knowledge can hardly be over-estimated, provided—but always provided— that it is not trusted too far. In the first flush of enthusiasm (as we have seen) it was thought capable of everything: to-day it remains to learn not its powers but its limitations. There is, in fact, another branch of knowledge to which critical analysis must inevitably be subordinated, the knowledge not merely of the psychology of the writers but of the historical conditions in which, and of which, they wrote. More and more, as we scrutinize these books of the Old Testament, the need for this knowledge becomes not only obvious but urgent. Without it, it is no exaggeration to say that we are helpless, and that it would be better to abandon our researches altogether if we can find no better solution than one which traverses the whole tenor of Israelite Tradition.

But here again a warning must be uttered; for the method which we are to employ of testing the Biblical documents assumes as its basis a radical and absolute scepticism. It is no more prepared to accept the credentials of those sources which can be proved the earliest in point of date than it is to credit the least reliable of the post-exilic additions.[1] If this attitude appears to some readers to be a disturbing one, it will be seen in the sequel to have abundant justification. Meanwhile it is perhaps wise to remind them that the *reality* of Inspiration is in no way denied or affected by it. The great—we might almost call it the inestimable—benefit which the 'Higher Criticism' has conferred upon Christians is that it has delivered them for ever from the tyranny of the Infallible Pen. Whatever may be true of Mohammedans, of the descendants of the Old Israel, or even of our own immediate forefathers, the New Israel need no longer regard itself as the 'People of a Book', and can concentrate henceforth with a single-minded devotion upon its faith in, and allegiance to, a Person. Yet in spite of his refusal to accept the literal inerrancy of the Biblical documents, the Christian scholar can still treasure them as writings most wonderfully inspired by God, 'by divers portions and in divers manners', precisely because his grasp of the meaning of Inspiration has fastened on the deep, and not on the superficial, aspect of Truth. For it has been borne in upon him that the spiritual value of any

[1] It is not proposed to deal in detail with these 'priestly' redactions (p. 57, n. 1). The overwhelming evidence of their unhistorical character —their conflict with the statements of pre-exilic and even exilic prophets, &c.—is amply exposed in all commentaries (such as those of Driver and McNeile) and would extend this book beyond tolerable limits.

'holy' scripture need in no wise be impoverished by the material limitations of the scribe.

If these considerations are borne in mind, a scientific approach to the documents is at once made possible. *None* of these, not even those which can be proved to be the earliest, are to be trusted unreservedly in matters of historical detail. The reason for this is twofold. There is, in the first place, the obvious fact that these documents were not composed at all till many centuries after the events which they describe; and these centuries, so far from being barren of incident, were among the most eventful in the history of the Nation. That the picture of the remote Past which is here exhibited has been entirely uninfluenced by those more recent vicissitudes of Israel may be regarded as frankly inconceivable. But there is another and a far weightier reason for approaching its details with a profound scepticism; and this lies in the strong 'aetiological' tendency which pervades the whole 'historical' literature of the ancient world.

Aetiology should properly be defined as 'the science of detecting underlying purposes or causes', whether in human life or in Nature; and in this sense the method which is to be employed below can be correctly described as 'aetiological'. But the word is also used of those ancient writers who, if they could not discover the true explanation of some fact or event of their experience, were accustomed to supply one out of their own heads. This tendency is particularly observable in the Book of Genesis where no less than five distinct classes of 'aetiological' story have been noted.[1] They are (1) *ethnic* (i.e.

---

[1] Lods, pp. 153–6. It is to be regretted that he has not realized the need for the same test in Exodus and Numbers.

designed to explain tribal or national relationships);
(2) *legal* (to validate some claim, as, e.g. to the wells of
Beersheba); (3) *etymological* (a fanciful interpretation of
place-names with the object of bringing them into line
with some supposed event); (4) *cultural* (to account for
a religious custom, for the sanctity of some particular
place or object, &c.); (5) *geographical* (to explain the
unusual appearance of some district, &c.). With certain
modifications all these types of aetiology are to be observed in the Books of Exodus and Numbers; the only
essential difference being that, whereas the stories of the
earlier book are based on the patriarchal age, in the latter
the reference is exclusively to the Events of the Exodus.
When we examine these later 'traditions', in short, we
find ourselves increasingly compelled to doubt their
historical worth. They are in no sense the Tradition
itself: very frequently they are not even embellishments
of it: they are Sacred Stories (ἱεροὶ λόγοι) designed for
specific purposes; and in no one absolutely clear instance
is the purpose to be recognized as what *we* should call
historical.

If this conclusion seems at first sight to preclude all
hope of arriving at the facts, in reality it carries us towards
them; for the memory of the Past upon which these
writers built was the sole condition of their being able
to write at all. Not even the 'priestly' editors of the post-
exilic age can be accused of basing what they teach upon
a foundation which they know to be nebulous. On the
contrary, it was precisely because they accepted the
essential elements of the Tradition (and amongst them
we must at least include the figures of Moses and Aaron,
and the Sacred Ark and Tent of Meeting) that they found
it possible to proclaim their own special message through

the symbolism of these immemorial forms. And what is
true of these is evidently even more true of their much
earlier predecessors. However much they may embellish
the facts, or even obscure them in the interests of their
particular purpose, at the heart of their narrative these
facts remain as a solid, resistant core, the indestruc-
tible nucleus of historical reality, without which there
would have been neither Scripture, nor symbolism, nor
Inspiration. In a word, the facts are *there*, though they
may not be by any means recognizable in the *form* in
which they are presented: they are there, but we shall
not discover them until we have penetrated *behind* the
immediate purpose of the individual writer and the garb
in which he has clothed it.[1]

Two examples of the aetiological method may be
given here which will serve to illustrate the force of this
contention and the general line of approach to the documents which it is proposed to follow hereafter. They will
be useful, at the same time, in exposing in its most
extreme form the radical contrast which exists between
the conclusions of this method and those of an unassisted
textual analysis.

There are two points about the story of the Exodus on
which many modern scholars appear to have reached a
general agreement. The first of them is the belief that
Kadesh, not the Mount of God, was the real centre at
which the religion of Jahweh was founded; the other
that this religion was originally that of the Midianites
(or Kenites) and was received by them from Moses
through the instructions of his father-in-law Jethro (or
Hobab). Whether, indeed, it is necessary to assume any

[1] Cf. Lods, p. 153.

historical basis in the story of the events at Sinai (or Horeb) is a matter about which there is still a variety of opinion. In the view of some critics, this is the invention of a later age: others suggest that the mountain may have been visited by *Moses*, but not by his people: others again are prepared to defend the tradition as authentic.[1] As it will, fortunately, be unnecessary to enter the dust of this arena, a closer inspection of the combatants can be dispensed with: it need only be said that the views which have here been described in general terms are founded upon two alleged episodes in the Wanderings; the water-miracle located at Meribah of Kadesh and narrated both *before* and *after* the sojourn at the Mount of God, and the visit of Jethro to Moses after the arrival of Israel at that mountain. It is these two episodes which have now to be examined.

1. THE EPISODE OF THE WATER-MIRACLE.

In the earlier passage in which this miracle is recorded (Exod. xvii. 1–7), we are told that *"there was no water for the people to drink. Wherefore the people strove with Moses . . . And Moses said unto them, Why strive ye with me? Wherefore do ye tempt Jahweh? . . . And Jahweh said unto Moses,*

> *Pass on before the people, and take with thee of the elders of Israel; and thy rod, wherewith thou smotest the river, take in thine hand and go. Behold, I will stand before thee there upon the rock in Horeb; and thou shalt smite the rock, and there shall come water out of it, that the people may drink."*

[1] The views of the earlier critics are ably summarized by R. Weill (*Le Séjour des Israelites au Desert et le Sinai*, 1909, pp. 15–36). Of recent writers, Olmstead follows Hölscher in the more extreme school of thought; Gressmann thinks Sinai a volcano visited by Moses; Lods follows Meyer *et al.* in practically identifying Sinai and Kadesh (p. 175); Robinson holds the conservative belief in a Sinai, but does not regard its position as important (p. 83).

Having accomplished the miracle Moses named the place *Massah* (i.e. 'Tempting"), and *Meribah* (i.e. 'Striving'),

> "*because of the striving of the children of Israel, and because they tempted Jahweh, saying, Is Jahweh among us, or not?*"

It should be noted that in this account the miracle is located somewhere in the neighbourhood of Horeb, which the Israelites are now supposed to be approaching. No closer indication of its whereabouts is provided by the earlier source (or sources), nor is there any suggestion that it was connected with Kadesh. The reference to Rephidim in the first verse of the chapter is a recognizable interpolation of the priestly school, while the Rephidim-battle against Amalek which immediately follows the miracle is equally recognizable as an isolated fragment, belonging in all probability to the last years of the Wandering.[1]

Deferring comment for the moment, we may pass to the later passage (Num. xx. 2–13). Here the miracle is explicitly located at *Kadesh*. The people 'strive' with Moses: Moses and Aaron present themselves before the door of the Tent of Meeting; and the Glory of Jahweh appears to them. Moses is commanded to take the rod, and after assembling the congregation with Aaron his brother to "*speak to the rock*" before their eyes. He obeys the first part of the command, but infringes the second. With the cry,

> "*Hear now, ye rebels; shall we bring you forth water out of this rock?*"

he lifts up his hand and smites the rock twice so that the water comes forth abundantly. The narrative continues:

[1] McNeile, p. 102.

"*And Jahweh said unto Moses and Aaron, Because ye believed not in me, to* SANCTIFY *me in the eyes of the children of Israel, therefore ye shall not bring this assembly into the land which I have given them.*

These are the waters of Meribah; because the children of Israel STROVE *with Jahweh and he was* SANCTIFIED *in them.*"

These last words are repeated later when Moses is commanded to ascend the mountain of Abarim and take his first and last view of the Promised Land:

"*And when thou hast seen it, thou also shalt be gathered unto thy people, as Aaron thy brother was gathered: because ye rebelled against my word in the wilderness of Zin, in the* STRIFE *of the congregation, to* SANCTIFY *me at the waters before their eyes.*

(*These are the waters of Meribah* [STRIVING] *of Kadesh* [SANCTIFY] *in the wilderness of Zin.*)"[1]

In examining these two accounts we receive a useful object lesson both in the strength and in the limitations of textual analysis. There can be no question, thanks to the power that it has given us of discriminating between the various documentary sources, that the miracle which is here related twice, as if it occurred on two different occasions (and in two different places?), is in reality one and the same. This is now universally accepted and it is superfluous to dwell on it. It need only be added that the first of these passages gives an account the groundwork of which is of comparatively early date; while the other is derived largely if not entirely from a 'priestly' source which is decidedly later.

So far the analysis of the documents can carry us with complete certainty, but now it begins to hesitate. That

[1] Num. xxvii. 13–14.

there are two strands in the earlier passage, the one associated with the name Massah, the other with that of Meribah, is sufficiently obvious; but there is considerable disagreement about the sources to which each of these belongs.[1] Finally, from this point onwards the analysis is powerless to help us. On the really vital question as to which, if any, of the three sources is the most reliable, it has nothing to say. To determine *this* problem is, in fact, entirely outside its scope; for even if it could prove beyond a doubt which of the earlier narrative-forms was actually the more ancient, it would still not follow that this form was—simply on that account—the nearest to the truth.

Some other test is evidently needed, and here the aetiological method comes into play:

(i) The most suspicious element in the whole of these two (or three) narratives is the precise location of the miracle at *Meribah of Kadesh*. There are, in fact, two obvious aetiological factors at work here, the *geographical* and the *etymological*. Exactness of topographical detail in the midst of an ancient legend stands self-condemned as historically worthless: it merely means that some one is interested in identifying a place which is actually known to him and his readers, with the site of the great event which he is describing. The analogy of the mysterious isle of Avalon so adroitly identified with the actual hill of Glastonbury is an example which leaps to the mind. There are, of course, numberless others. Now it is clear from the expression: "*These are the waters of Meribah of Kadesh in the wilderness of Zin*" that the writer is drawing attention to a place which must be familiar to

---

[1] Thus Driver and McNeile assign *Massah* to J and *Meribah* to E while Gressmann and Procksch exactly reverse this.

his countrymen, and this is confirmed by Ezekiel, who uses it as one of the landmarks on the map of his southern border of Israel:

> "*The south side southward shall be from Tamar as far as the waters of Meriboth-kadesh . . .*"[1]

Moreover it can be shown that this Kadesh (which is the Kadesh-barnea of the earlier documents) is undoubtedly to be identified with the High Places of Petra (Sela, Joktheel);[2] and that the 'waters' are those of the Wady Musa which flow through the narrow and precipitous chasm of the Sik. It needs no straining of the imagination to conceive of this chasm having been created by the slashing downstroke of the wonder-working Rod of Moses, and this alone must have made the identification easy. (It must be remembered that for two fairly long periods the Israelites were in possession of the Arabah and either friendly with the inhabitants of Sela or in actual possession of that stronghold.)[3] Lastly, there is the *etymological* 'explanation' of the two names, neither of which, it hardly needs saying, can have had anything to do with Moses or ancient Israel. If there is, in short, one overwhelmingly certain conclusion to be drawn, it is that the whole of this account is worthless as historical evidence.

(ii) What then of the *Meribah* parallel in the earlier narrative? This need not detain us long. The fact that the critics themselves are not agreed about its origin is a clear indication that the characteristics of a particular

---

[1] Ezek. xlvii. 19; xlviii. 28; cf. Deut. xxxii. 51 (P).

[2] See below p. 195, Appendix I. (The existence of a supposed 'Holy' spring in the Negeb was refuted by Lawrence in 1914. Ain Kadeis means the 'spring of the wooden paddle'.)

[3] See below Appendix I.

source are wanting. There is, in fact, no reason at all why this 'parallel' should not be—what for other reasons we might naturally expect it to be—an interpolation on the part of the 'priestly' redactor himself. Finding a water-miracle already fixed in this early position, but related not to Meribah of Kadesh but to an unknown Massah, he assumed the scene of both to be the same. He therefore 'reconciled' the two accounts by introducing his Meribah and his 'striving' by the side of the more primitive Massah and 'tempting'. This appears to be the most obvious explanation; but it is, of course, possible that the Meribah of this account goes back to Solomonic times when the identification of the miracle site with the Wadi Musa was probably first made. In any event the etymological aetiology of the name condemns it as untrustworthy, and we can dismiss it from our calculations.

(iii) Is *Massah*, in turn, an original element of the Tradition? This, too, seems to be inadmissible; not only on the score of aetiology but because in the Blessing of Moses (Deut. xxxiii) this name receives an entirely different interpretation and is referred to an entirely different episode! It appears there not as a shameful, but as a most honourable, memory, which recalls how, when the priestly tribe of Levi was '*tested*' by Jahweh, it emerged victorious from the ordeal.[1] The occasion alluded to seems to be that in which the Levites championed the cause of Jahweh by a ruthless slaughter of their own kinsmen, when the weakness of Aaron had

[1] Deut. xxxiii. 8. Here again the 'priestly' redactor's hand seems to have interpolated after *Massah* the inevitable *Meribah*; for the explanation of this name, "*With whom thou (Jahweh) dost strive,*" is quite incongruous with the honorific interpretation of *Massah*. For the date of the Blessing (the reign of Saul) see below p. 101.

brought disgrace upon Israel.[1] This episode in the form in which we now have it has been 'toned down', presumably out of a growing reverence for Aaron;[2] and it is probable that the reference to Massah as the 'test' by which Levi won the priesthood was dropped out as a part of this process. The name itself, however, may have become too familiar by this time to be forgotten: it was therefore transferred with a different interpretation to the water-miracle 'at the rock in Horeb' from which the original name was in turn removed.[3] All this will probably strike the reader as the wildest guesswork, and he must be asked to suspend judgement till the full evidence is examined in a later chapter. Here it is only necessary to insist that a name which has inspired two completely opposite etymological interpretations can scarcely claim to be an undisturbed portion of the original foundations!

(iv) Finally, then, we are left with the 'rock in Horeb' itself. This is not yet the irreducible minimum to which we can descend; for we must be prepared to find ourselves left with the bare fact, that Moses struck a rock somewhere in the wilderness and produced water from it. There appears, however, no valid reason for rejecting the reference to Horeb. Whether the general position

---

[1] Exod. xxxii. 26–8. A full discussion of this highly complicated mosaic of legends is given below pp. 108 ff. The small fragment, Exod. xv. 25, seems to have been broken away from the same context.

[2] That Jahweh was 'very angry' with Aaron and would have destroyed him but for the intercession of Moses is stated in Deut. ix. 20, but there is no sign of it in the corresponding narrative of Exodus. But it is impossible to follow these shifts of attitude without a thorough comprehension of the vicissitudes of the Priesthood in historical times.

[3] The word 'there' (Exod. xvii. 6) presupposes the mention of a place which has disappeared from the text.

of the mountain was or was not known in historical times,[1] it was at any rate remote in the popular imagination;[2] and we can imagine no special motive for telling stories about it. There seems, in fact, no reason why the event should have been recorded in this form except to preserve the memory of the miracle: for the reference to Horeb seems to be purely incidental and is, just for that reason, the more likely to be authentic. As to whether the remaining details of the story, the 'passing on before the people', the escort of elders, &c., are equally to be trusted, we have no means of deciding. *Once for all we must realize that it is useless to press the minutiae of the documentary evidence where no external proofs are available for their verification.* The semblance of a sharply defined Reality which these records dangle before our eyes is, in effect, a mirage which has already beguiled too many over-trustful explorers. Rather than share their fate, we shall content ourselves with broader and less disputable conclusions; and all that seems warrantable here is that *the Basis of the Tradition did definitely record the working of this miracle by Moses after the Exodus, and that it took place, most probably, in the vicinity of Horeb the Mount of God.*[3]

2. THE EPISODE OF JETHRO'S VISIT. (Exod. xviii. 1–27.)

This episode is divided into two scenes which are in the closest association (a fact which seems sometimes to be overlooked). In the *first* scene Jethro, the priest of

---

[1] A note in Deut. i. 2 gives the distance from Horeb to Kadesh-barnea as 11 days' journey, but it is impossible to say on what data the calculation was based.

[2] Cf. Elijah's journey of '40 days and 40 nights' from Beersheba to Horeb (1 Kings xix. 3–8).

[3] An instance of a 'great gush of clear water' being liberated from the rock by two blows of a shovel is recorded by Major C. S. Jarvis, Governor of Sinai (*Yesterday and To-day in Sinai*, 1931, p. 174).

Midian, Moses' father-in-law, having heard all that God has done for Moses seeks him out at his encampment at the Mount of God. There Moses relates to him all that Jahweh has done to Pharaoh and the Egyptians for Israel's sake; and Jethro on hearing this pronounces the following eulogy:

"Blessed be Jahweh, who hath delivered you out of the hand of the Egyptians, and out of the hand of Pharaoh. . . .
Now I know that Jahweh is greater than all gods:
Yea, in the thing wherein they dealt proudly against them."

He then offers a *"burnt-offering and sacrifices for God"*, and Aaron and all the elders of Israel come and eat bread with him solemnly *"before God"* (i.e. at the Sanctuary, which is supposed by this time to exist).

The general meaning of this passage is so clear that it seems hardly credible that any one should mistake it. There is nothing here to suggest that Jahweh is the god of Midian and that Jethro is His priest:[1] on the contrary it is precisely because He is *not* the god of Midian that the emphasis is laid on the fact that Jethro himself was 'priest of Midian'. The whole story up to this point is written to magnify Jahweh, Whose great deeds, as related by Moses, entirely convince the priest of *another* religion that the God of Moses is *"greater than all gods"*. It then goes on to tell how Jethro, not content with this oral declaration of faith, confirmed it by action: he testified his new allegiance to Jahweh by offering Him sacrifices. Finally, now that he had become linked with Israel by this irrevocable act, he was admitted to a solemn feast of fellowship with the leading representatives of the Nation.

---

[1] It is surely inconceivable that even if this had actually been the fact it would have been allowed to appear in the records of Israel.

(He was already in special relationship to Moses, so that it is Aaron and the elders who now come forward in that role.)

This is unquestionably the meaning of the whole scene, for an exact parallel is to be found in the story of Naaman. Here, too, a foreigner is 'converted' to Jahweh by the great things which He has done; and the first requirement of this new allegiance is a load of Israelite earth on which the proper "*burnt-offerings and sacrifices*" can be offered to Jahweh in Syria.[1]

But if this is the meaning, what is the *object*, of the story? Here again there seems little room for doubt. Its real object is not merely to magnify Jahweh, but to prepare the way for what follows. We come then to the *second* scene of the episode.

On the following day, we are told, Jethro stood watching while Moses judged the people and gave them the statutes and laws of God, a process which on account of their numbers went on continuously from morning until evening. Afterwards he remonstrated with his son-in-law for attempting an impossible task, and advised him to organize the whole people into thousands, hundreds, fifties, and tens, appointing men of special character and ability as group-officers and judges, and retaining only the harder causes for his own decision. This suggestion was welcomed and immediately followed out by Moses, while Jethro departed to his own land.

The object of the *first* scene is now apparent: it is to show that Jethro had secured the *necessary qualifications* for offering this practical but revolutionary piece of advice. Had he not been previously admitted to the fellowship of Israel, his counsel would have been rejected,

[1] 2 Kings v. 17.

if not by Moses, yet certainly by the people at large: it would, in fact, have been an impertinence on his part to offer it. As it was, though still a foreigner, he was by confession and act a Jahwist, and the benefits of his wisdom might be welcomed and enjoyed by the Chosen People.

What, then, is the object of the episode as a whole? It is impossible to answer this question without having recourse to the facts of history; for it becomes necessary to ask when, if ever, such an organization of justice existed. It was certainly unknown in Israel at the time of Absalom's rebellion; for we are told that one of the chief causes of discontent of which he took skilful advantage was that *"no man was deputed of the king"* to hear the causes of the tribesmen.[1] But it is possible to go a little farther than this. In a strongly anti-monarchical utterance which is put into the mouth of Samuel, the people are warned of the kind of thing they will have to endure when they have a king to reign over them; and amongst their grievances is included the fact that he will take their sons for *"captains of thousands and captains of fifties."*[2] Now the whole of this passage reads like a vigorous attack on Solomon; for it emphasizes the impressing of the people for forced labour and the demand for the tenth of their seed, vineyards, and flocks; details which are omitted in the somewhat similar 'prophecy' in Deuteronomy, written presumably when the power of the king had been crippled.[3] It may be suggested, then, that the 'numbering of the people', which ended so disastrously in David's reign, was undertaken for the specific purpose of establishing some such new judicial

[1] 2 Sam. xv. 2–4.   [2] 1 Sam. viii. 12.
[3] Deut. xvii. 14–20; cf. Smith, *Samuel*, 1912, p. 55 f.

organization, and that it was actually carried into effect, along with other drastic innovations, by Solomon. That it would be intensely unpopular goes without saying. The immemorial 'units' of the Near East are the family, the village, the clan, the tribe; and this soulless and unprecedented mathematical substitute must have aroused, for all its usefulness, a hostility both secular and religious.

But is it possible to go yet a step farther, and to suppose that this new and complicated scheme of administration was *borrowed* by Solomon from one of those more highly developed civilizations with which he was on terms of intimate friendship; from Phoenicia, for example, or even from Egypt itself? Is it not, in fact, conceivable that the idea of it was suggested to him by the rulers of one of these countries: and that when it had been accepted by him and applied in Israel the knowledge of its foreign origin brought down upon it the vehement wrath of all good Jahwists? It is certainly curious that the term "*father-in-law*" occurs no less than thirteen times in this one short episode: it suggests that the fact of this relationship was being stressed deliberately by the writer. Had he in mind the state visit to Jerusalem of one of these monarchs, coming to congratulate his son-in-law on the prosperity which Jahweh had given him, and to offer a diplomatic sacrifice on the great altar of the new Temple?

If these conjectures appear too imaginative, they are not for that reason to be dismissed with impatience or contempt. Whatever facts inspired the writing of this episode, they are the facts of an historical period long subsequent to the age of Moses, and the episode itself was composed, it can scarcely be doubted, to provide an explanation of them, if not an apologia. It is an attempt, in short, such as we often find in these books, to cast the sanction of the Past over events or institutions of a much later day; and, while it may be based on the memory of services rendered to Moses and his people in the wilderness by the kinsfolk of his wife, it is itself devoid of even the faintest shadow of historical reality. Even the name Jethro, indeed, appears to be a pure invention. In the earlier scenes in Midian when Moses first meets this 'priest of Midian', he is described quite simply as 'the man';[1] and it is doubtful whether he was originally named here at all: certainly whenever a name appears in these earlier passages, the Greek versions vary between Jothor (Jethro) and Ragouel (Reuel) and between 'father-in-law' and 'brother-in-law'.[2] Three stages are, in fact, apparent; the first in which the priest is nameless; the second in which he is called Reuel and becomes the father-in-law of Moses; the third in which the new name of Jethro having been interpolated, an effort is made to reconcile his relationship with both Reuel and Moses. (In Numbers yet a fourth stage appears with Hobab, who is the son of Reuel and who may actually have rendered the services, the memory of which inspired the inventor of Jethro.)[3] Nothing could betray more clearly the historical worthlessness of this 'tradition': but its examination has at least enabled us to draw one important *negative* conclusion: *that there is no particle of evidence to be found here for assuming that Moses derived his religion from a priest of Midian.*

These illustrations have been chosen to fulfil a twofold purpose in clearing the way to a more penetrating study of the documents. On the one hand they serve to reveal the inherent weakness of the 'scissors and paste' method,

---

[1] Exod. ii. 21.   [2] Exod. ii. 16–18; iii. 1.   [3] Num. x. 29–32.

which seeks to piece together the largest possible 'historical' picture out of the greatest possible number of the earliest possible documentary fragments, while completely ignoring their aetiological significance. On the other hand, they will have indicated (it is hoped) what must be the next and indispensable step in our undertaking. It will be evident that the application of the aetiological method virtually necessitates the posing and answering in each case of three questions:

(i) Why was this written down?
(ii) When?
(iii) By whom?

Not all these questions can be answered in every instance; but they hang so close together that where the first of them proves amenable the others will often follow automatically, if only in the most general terms. What is, however, much more to the present purpose is that they form together one compact historical problem, and that they can only be answered when sufficient historical data are available. Unfortunately this is just where the chief difficulty lies. The narratives of the books of Samuel and Kings are perhaps the least trustworthy of any 'historical' treatises in existence for the simple reason that they were never composed for the sake of recording history. Great figures such as Samuel are haloed in legendary glamour, others like Saul are obscured by deliberate obloquy; while events of far-reaching significance are ignored or dismissed with the briefest mention. Nowhere, in short, is there greater need for the revaluation both of the chief actors and of their achievements; for the reconstruction of the true historical sequences of cause and effect; for the continual use of that imaginative insight which will dare to ignore the written words, and to decipher the palimpsest which they have almost obliterated. Unfortunately, once more, such a study of Israelite history has yet to be written (for even the massive work of Rudolf Kittel falls short of what is demanded). If, therefore, some attempt is to be made in the following pages to follow this bewildering and tangled trail, its obvious imperfections may justly plead for sympathy. For the attempt *must* be made. Until we have understood the successive crises through which Jahwism passed, from the humble sanctuary at Shiloh to the gorgeous fane which shone above the roofs of Zion, we shall fail to grasp how inevitably some reflection of them must have been preserved by the Guardians of the basic Tradition of Israel.

Chapter II

THE GUARDIANS OF THE TRADITION

"RISE UP, JAHWEH, AND LET THINE ENEMIES BE SCATTERED. . . ."[1] By Araunah's threshing-floor, where it faces the old Jebusite ramparts and the great north gate of Zion, the veteran musters of Israel stand marshalled tribe by tribe, impatient for their commander to lead them again to victory. Year after year they have assembled on this well-worn ground, armed with a confidence which had made them long since invincible: year after year they have returned to it, laden with spoils and loud with their tales of triumph: year after year of unchecked and ever widening conquests, till the name and the prowess of David have inspired a universal terror, from the Field of Edom to the distant Hittite kingdoms that fringe Euphrates.

But it is not for David now that these warriors are waiting; for the ageing king rides out no more with his army: it is for the Leader, to whose power David himself is fain to ascribe his victories; the Leader whose glory is as far beyond his own as David himself outshines all earthly monarchs. And now that Leader comes. Through the wide-flung gate, as the chanting multitudes halt and part asunder, the Divine Palladium of Israel, shrouded and formidable, emerges: borne

---

[1] Cf. Num. x. 35–6. This battle-cry, alleged to have been used by Moses *"when the Ark set forward"*, is not in fact at home in the context of the Wanderings, while the greeting *"when it is rested"*, *"Return Jahweh to the thousands of the ten thousands of Israel"*, is even less appropriate. This fragment of ritual must belong to the only historical period when the Ark led Israel to the Wars, i.e. the reign of David. The imaginary scene described above is therefore not wholly conjectural.

shoulder-high, in the midst of Its priestly escort, the
Ark of God marches towards the Van. As It takes Its
accustomed place, the whole scene dissolves into martial
tumult. With a clash of arms the divisions close and
wheel after It: the trumpets blare: the white dust flies
into clouds in the stir of innumerable feet: from Kedron
to Olivet goes echoing, in jubilant thunder, the Battle
Hymn of Jahweh, Lord of the Hosts of Heaven:

> *"Let God arise, let his enemies be scattered;*
> *Let them also that hate him flee before him.*
>
> .   .   .   .
>
> *Sing unto God, sing praises to his name:*
> *Cast up a high way for him that rideth through the deserts;*
> *His name is* JAH; *and exult ye before him.*
>
> .   .   .   .
>
> *O God, when thou wentest forth before thy people,*
> *When thou didst march through the wilderness;*
> *The earth trembled,*
> *The heavens also dropped at the presence of God. . . ."*[1]

Some such effort of the imagination will surely win its
reward, if it quickens in us a sense of realities long
forgotten; if it provokes us, at the least, to demand by
what secret virtue this relic of the Past dominated the
dissensions of Israel. That the recovery of the Ark from
its obscure resting-place in Kirjath-jearim was, in the
event, the master-stroke of David's reign, is one of those
inferences which is as certain as it is incapable of proof.
In the narrative, even as it is spread before us, the alleged
alacrity of the northern tribes to receive back to their
hearts the father and conqueror of Absalom is hardly

[1] Ps. lxviii. 1, 4, 7–8.

supported by the almost immediate rebellion which threatened for a time to dissolve the unity of the Nation:[1] nor was it a mere impulsive reaction from the tyranny of Solomon which in the end 'rent the kingdom' irrecoverably from the House of David. The cause of both these revolts was one and the same. If the authority of Saul, the scion of insignificant Benjamin, was only grudgingly accepted by the pride of Ephraim, for so long the self-appointed leader of the Nation, the passing of the hegemony into the hands of Saul's former lieutenant, a half-Moabite upstart from a half-Edomite Judah, must have aroused in both these lately dominant tribes a fierce and inextinguishable jealousy. It can have been by no accident that the first of these uprisings was instigated by the Benjamite Bichri, and the second by the Ephraimite Jeroboam: nor could any facts reveal more clearly the strength of those disruptive forces with which David had from the first to contend. That he not only contended with but triumphed over them, must surely be ascribed to the two great achievements by which his genius must for all time be measured; the establishment of a new capital in the neutral zone wrested so brilliantly from the Jebusites, and the enthronement in it of the Sacred Ark, the venerable symbol of Israel's unity. Which of these two was the more potent factor in his success is, again, hardly disputable: it was the act which at one blow extinguished the humiliation of a national disaster, revived in all breasts the glorious memories of the Exodus, and sent forth the armies of Israel, conquering and to conquer, under the aegis of a Divine Protection visible to every eye.

The Ark of God; what it was and what it held; its own

[1] 2 Sam. xx. 1–22.

fortunes and those of its sacred custodians—here, very evidently, must be the starting-point for any serious attempt to investigate the Tradition of Israel. For if the stories told about the Ark and its Priesthood have any substance, the clue to much that at present seems inexplicable in the confusions and contradictions of the written documents must surely be lying hidden in the tale of their vicissitudes.

When a nation claims to possess not merely a sacred cult-object but a sacerdotal caste in immemorial charge of it, it is no more than reasonable to assume that the tradition of its origin will have been preserved in its essentials by these guardians.

When, further, it is related that this sacred object was at one time ignominiously captured by the enemy; that, when returned to its owners, it was allowed by them to languish in obscurity for many years; and that, in spite of this loss and this subsequent indifference, a central sanctuary was still maintained through the whole of the period, with a priesthood which still performed its customary duties, it may be regarded as highly probable that these striking changes will have left their marks indelibly imprinted on the records.

When, finally, we are told that this hereditary priestly caste was practically extinguished in bloodshed and that the sacred office was committed, at first temporarily and afterwards permanently, into other hands, it may be anticipated that this too will have left its traces behind.

Our first step, then, will be to examine whatever evidence is available on the history of the Ark and its Priesthood, and to construct out of it, with the aid of our mother-wit, a sufficiently probable picture of what actually occurred. A comparison of this picture with the stories told in the Books of Exodus and Numbers should then reveal some at least of the underlying reasons for their inconsistencies.

1. THE ARK AND ITS CONTENTS

As to this, in spite of a great variety of theories,[1] there is actually not much that need be said. When the Ark was deposited with all solemnity in the inner shrine of Solomon's Temple it was believed to contain *"the two tables of stone which Moses put there at Horeb"*.[2] Whether this was actually the case or not—and this remains to be explored later—there can be no doubt at all that it represents the unvarying Israelite conviction. According to this, the Ark was a chest constructed specially by Moses to hold two tables of stone,[3] and it was these which gave it its supernatural sanctity. There is, it is true, a very formidable difficulty here, but it is not one that need be discussed at the moment. It is sufficient to hold fast the golden rule that *a prevailing tradition should be accepted provisionally, in its bare essentials, unless and until there is*

[1] The literature is voluminous. Among the theories advanced by scholars the following may be mentioned: (1) that the Ark contained a meteorite (Stade), a Fetish-stone (Vatke, Benzinger, Duhm, Holzinger, Marti), stones taken from the Mount of God (Moore, Robinson, Driver (?)); (2) that it contained a Bull-image (Gressmann), the Brazen Serpent (Kennett), symbols of the Osiris cult or the bones of Joseph (Procksch); (3) that it was an (empty) throne (Schwally, Voltz, Reichel, Meinhold, Gunkel, Dibelius, Kittel). Dibelius regards it as Babylonian in origin, Stade and Hartmann as Canaanite, Gressmann as Midianite or Kenite, Procksch as a cult-object of the Joseph tribes, Hölscher as belonging to the southern tribes, Westphal as an importation from Asia Minor. For references and discussion, see Driver, *Exodus*, 1918, p. 278 f.; McNeile, p. 161 f.; Oesterley and Robinson, *Hebrew Religion*, 1930, p. 144; Kittel, *Geschichte des Volkes Israel*, 1923, I, p. 374; Westphal, *Jahwes Wohnstatten*, 1908, p. 90; Hölscher, *Gesch. der israelitischen u. jüdischen Religion*, 1922, p. 22; Procksch, *Die Elohimquelle*, 1906, p. 374.

[2] 1 Kings viii. 9.　　　　　[3] Deut. x. 1–3.

tangible evidence to disprove it. In this instance no such evidence is forthcoming. It may be highly probable, it may indeed be certain, that the Solomonic tables of stone were neither of the age nor of the origin ascribed to them; but it is not what they were, but what they were believed to be that is all-important; since it is the existence of this unchallenged belief which must determine our general conception of the Ark and its purpose. It may be assumed, then, that the Ark was originally revered not for its own sake but for the objects which it contained; and that these objects were *originally* two fragments of stone, which were regarded as so 'permeated', in some mysterious way, with the abiding Power of Jahweh that they represented His actual Presence (*Panim*) amongst His People.

2. The Priesthood of Shiloh

The early chapters of the first book of Samuel are unfortunately very far from being trustworthy historical records, and this is more especially true of those parts of them which deal with Shiloh and its Priesthood. With whatever original purpose these were written they bear obvious traces now of aetiological colouring: they are concerned, in short, to explain why the Ark was lost and why the descendants of Eli were pursued by consistent misfortune. Nor is this colouring a friendly one, as a single example will show. The prediction by an unknown 'man of God' of the disasters which would befall the Elidae (1 Sam. ii. 27–36) has been thoroughly edited, if not entirely composed, by a partisan of the Zadokite house which succeeded them. In its original form this prophecy may have ended with the first part of verse 33, which should be translated: "*Yet* ONE *I will not cut off belonging to thee from mine altar*"; the reference being in the first place to Ahitub, Ichabod's brother, and, in the second, to Abiathar who alone survived the massacre of Nob. As it now stands, however, the humiliation of the Elidae is described as *complete*, and the reference to Zadok as their supplanter is quite unmistakable:

> "*And I will raise me up a faithful priest, that shall do according to that which is in mine heart and in my mind: and he shall walk before mine anointed for ever.*"[1]

The importance of this conclusion becomes clear when we approach the difficult question of Eli's ancestry. In the opening words of the prophecy already mentioned there is this remarkable statement:

> "*Thus saith Jahweh,*
> *Did I reveal myself unto the house of thy father, when they were in Egypt in bondage to Pharaoh's house? And did I choose him out of all the tribes of Israel to be my priest . . .?*"[2]

When it is remembered that the writer (or editor) of this was definitely hostile to the Elidae, it will be realized that here at least we have to do with a reliable tradition. There can have been no object in allowing such an assertion to stand, if it had not contained a truth which it was idle to tamper with. It must be assumed, then, that the family of Eli was none other than the hereditary priesthood of Mosaic days, and there is a further possibility that it may have been established in this office even before the departure of Israel from Egypt.[3]

But what priesthood could this have been but that of Aaron? It is, of course, not enough to answer that this

---

[1] Steuernagel, 'Die Weissagung über die Eliden', in *Altt. Stud.*, 1913, pp. 204 ff.; Driver, *Notes on the Hebrew Text of the Books of Samuel*, 1913, *ad loc.*   [2] I Sam. ii. 27-8.   [3] See above, p. 51.

was never doubted in Israel; for we have really no certain evidence of this belief beyond the post-exilic views of the 'priestly' writers.[1] *Then* the Aaronic priesthood was not only assumed but elevated to a ruling dogma; but it by no means follows that this was true of any earlier period. It is certain that Ezekiel himself knows nothing of it: for him the high-priestly house is that of the Zadokites.[2] And what is true of Ezekiel is presumably even more true of the founder of that house himself, who, so far from requiring an ancestry, provided one.

There are, however, two details which seem to point directly to the origin of Eli's family and these are the (apparently) Egyptian names of his two sons Hophni and Phinehas,[3] and the fact that the second of these was borne by the famous grandson of Aaron himself.[4] Neither of these amounts to a proof; but if the presumption be accepted provisionally it will be found to explain much which in the present documents of the Tradition is otherwise incomprehensible. It provides us, in short, with a period in Israelite history when the name of Aaron, though too deeply rooted and prominent in the memory of Israel to be eliminated, passed temporarily under a cloud. The ancestor had been disgraced in his lineage and the sins of the children were visited on the father.[5]

3. THE CAPTURE AND RETURN OF THE ARK

The relevant facts, though familiar, must be briefly related.[6] We are told that the Ark was carried out from Shiloh to hearten the Israelite army after an initial defeat

---

[1] The fact that the last re-editing of our document was done by these writers makes it impossible to accept any pro-Aaronic allusions as prior to their day.   [2] Ezek. xl. 46 *et pass.*
[3] Kittel, I, p. 373.   [4] Joshua xxiv. 33 ("the hill of P.").
[5] See below, p. 113 f.   [6] 1 Sam. iv. 2–vii. 2.

by the Philistines. The battle was again joined and disaster followed, both Hophni and Phinehas being slain and the Ark itself captured. For seven months it remained in Philistine hands, and it is recorded that during this period its captors had cause to regret their triumph. The image of Dagon of Ashdod, to whose temple it was first brought, was found with its face to the ground and its head and hands cut off; and the city itself was smitten with a sudden and terrible plague. Ashdod was in no doubt as to the cause of these calamities and sent the Ark to Gath: the plague followed it. From Gath it was passed hurriedly to Ekron: the plague still followed. The inhabitants of Ekron were in despair; "*for there was a deadly discomfiture throughout all the city*". It was resolved then that the Ark must be returned to Israel, with a golden guilt-offering to propitiate its outraged God. It was accordingly placed on a wagon and sent back "*by the way of its own border to Beth-shemesh*", where it was joyfully received. Beth-shemesh itself, however, was not to escape unscathed, for it is related that a large number of its people were smitten, because they looked into (or gazed at) the Ark.[1] In the end it was carried up into the mountains to the old Hivite stronghold of Kirjath-jearim, and there it remained in the house of one Abinadab for over fifty years.[2]

This neglect of the Ark after its victorious return has been rightly described as 'one of the most singular circumstances of a singular age'.[3] Indeed, if we assume that the narrative is substantially true—and there seems

---

[1] 1 Sam. vi. 19 (Driver, *Notes &c.*, p. 58).

[2] The *twenty years* of 1 Sam. vii. 2 cannot possibly be correct. Saul's reign alone must have been nearer 20 years than 15. Kittel (II, p. 215) dates the battle of Aphek 1080 and David's accession 1012 B.C.

[3] Kennedy, *Samuel* (The Century Bible), p. 325.

no reason to doubt it—its deliberate abandonment in the very moment of triumph seems at first sight entirely inexplicable. It has been suggested that Kirjath-jearim was already at this date under Philistine jurisdiction and that therefore the Ark was never really recovered at all.[1] But the only records we have speak most distinctly of its being restored to "*its own border*", which at this time seems to have run due north and south along the Shephelah. At Beth-shemesh it was already within Israelite territory, and the most obvious explanation of its removal to Kirjath-jearim lies in the desire for its greater safety. Beth-shemesh, though walled, was a small lowland town, directly exposed to a Philistine attack; while Kirjath-jearim, crowning the mountain tops 2,000 ft. above it, was one of the few great fortresses which had passed into Israelite hands.[2]

Some better explanation is clearly to be looked for; and since it is in the highest degree unlikely that anything derogatory to the Ark would be left in the narrative by those who restored it to its glory, it becomes an inevitable necessity to look for it 'between the lines'. Now it is assumed, on the strength of the later history of the Ark, that it returned to Israel in the same condition in which it was captured. But this is an assumption which a little reflection will show to be unwarranted. When David, in his turn, captured the 'gods' of the Philistines at Baal Perazim, he "*burned them*", according to the Chronicler, "*with fire*".[3] It was the natural act of a conqueror; and it is hardly conceivable that the Philistines themselves,

---

[1] Ib., pp. 217 ff., 325. Kittel suggests that the Ark was 'profaned' by its sojourn in Philistia (II, pp. 74, 120).

[2] Joshua ix. 17. The only Hivite city which has been excavated is Tell-el-Nasbeh (Beeroth): its walls were of colossal height and thickness.

[3] 1 Chron. xiv. 8 f. (cf. 2 Sam. v. 17 f.).

in the hour of their triumph over the dreaded "*gods of Israel*", would have left these "*gods*" intact. Savage and instant destruction is, in fact, the only sequel to be expected; and it is probable that the narrator himself knew that this vengeance had been wreaked. Was it merely for the capture of the Ark that the image of Dagon was *smashed in pieces?* Was it only for this reason that Philistia was decimated by plague? Was it for no greater sin that the golden guilt-offerings were presented? Surely in the mind of the writer, even though he does not, and perhaps dare not, express it, there lies behind the description of these events the feeling that Jahweh must avenge Himself for some far more deadly outrage! Surely, after all, the restoration of the Ark was but a barren act of reparation, since the sacred objects which it had once contained had been ruthlessly ground to powder!

This explanation, which appears so obvious once it has been thought of, sheds a flood of light on the events that followed. It accounts in the first place for the mysterious story of the smiting of the men of Beth-shemesh who may have displayed a profane curiosity as to whether or not the Ark was empty: but above all it explains why, so far from being borne back in triumph to lead the armies of Israel once more to victory, it was left silently in a private house, without ceremony or shrine or priesthood, to remain there for at least fifty years, derelict and forlorn.[1] Lastly, it must be noted as a very strong probability that this calamitous loss of the Sacred Stones must have left a deep imprint on the documents of the

---

[1] Eleazar ben Abinadab was appointed as caretaker, not as priest (1 Sam. vii. 1). Had he been a priest, his brother Uzzah would have been similarly consecrated and his fate otherwise interpreted (2 Sam. vi. 3 ff.).

Tradition. When David resolved to rehabilitate the Ark, this was the first and most formidable difficulty which he had to face. Some way, in fact, must be found whereby the magnitude of the disaster might be minimized; and this must have entailed a drastic modification of the original story.

4. THE PRIESTHOOD OF NOB

If the neglect of the Ark can be described as one of the most singular circumstances of that age, the triumphal survival of its empty sanctuary must be regarded as almost a miracle. The effect of the terrible disaster of Aphek can best be realized in the light of the years that followed; and these are revealed by the scanty evidence which survives as forming one of the most critical epochs in the history of the Nation. As the years passed, the Philistines gradually extended their suzerainty over Israel. They swarmed up over the mountains, destroyed Shiloh,[1] and held the main roads and passes with a chain of 'block-house' garrisons, so that any united effort at insurrection could be strangled at the birth. All weapons of war were forbidden, and lest there should be any attempt to beat plowshares into swords or pruning hooks into spears, not even a smithy was allowed "*in all the land of Israel*".[2] The situation, in short, must have seemed a wellnigh hopeless one, and it cannot be wondered at, if those who had seen the downfall of the national Palladium despaired of a struggle which must seem foredoomed to failure. 'Surely', many of them must have reasoned, 'we can look now no more for any help from

---

[1] This is the usual and most probable explanation of the desolation alluded to as a warning by Jeremiah (Jer. vii. 12, 14; xxvi. 6, 9).

[2] I Sam. xiii. 19 f.

Jahweh. Either He has deserted us in anger or He has proved powerless before the gods of the Philistines. Whatever be the cause, His Presence is no longer amongst us, for what is there now left to Israel but the mockery of an empty Shrine?' What followed can only be discerned with difficulty, but enough remains for us to piece some kind of picture together. Some part of the Hebrews (whether Israelites or near kinsmen) made terms with the Philistines and even accompanied them as camp-followers: others retired into the mountains and hid themselves in holes and caves: many more must have fled across Jordan and found a refuge amongst their brethren of Gilead.[1] Slowly, under the acid solvent of Philistine hegemony, the nation began to disintegrate; and even the boldest hearts must have wondered what the morrow would bring.

And then suddenly all was changed. A great wind of religious and national enthusiasm swept through the country. On every high road and through every village bands of young prophets, gripped by a mysterious ecstasy, roved up and down, kindling once more the fire of a patriotic zeal for Jahweh. Very soon the results of their preaching became evident. Voices were raised, crying out for a king to lead Israel against the enemy.[2] On all sides the national self-consciousness awoke from the torpor of despair.

What brought about this wonderful revival? There can be little doubt that it was, in the main, the work of a single man—Samuel. The legend of his miraculous defeat

[1] 1 Sam. xiv. 11, 21, 22; cf. 1 Sam. xxxi. 7—Saul's long-established connexion with Mahanaim favours this last hypothesis.

[2] The early narrative of 1 Sam. ix. 15 f. represents Saul as the divinely appointed ruler and saviour of Israel.

of the Philistines at Ebenezer[1] is valuable not as history (for it is contradicted by later events) but because it is a reflection of the man's real greatness as a national leader. Samuel was no warrior, but he was more: he was the great religious inspirer of Israel in this moment of crisis. That he was himself responsible for organizing the patriotic 'propaganda' of the prophets is highly probable. The scene at Naioth where we find a company of them prophesying *"and Samuel standing as head over them"*[2] may be imaginative, but it must surely be based on fact. It was Samuel, and Samuel only, who stood like a rock for Jahweh amidst the tides of the Philistine invasion.

This great revival of religious and patriotic zeal, to which was due the ultimate victory of Israel, could never have been brought about unless the disaster of the Ark had been repaired or its worst effects neutralized. But the disaster itself seemed final, for the Sacred Stones were gone: in what way, then, could confidence in Jahweh be restored? This was the dilemma which must have confronted Samuel. He himself, as a child, had been dedicated to Jahweh and had ministered day by day before His Ark:[3] in dreams and visions he had learned to feel His Presence and to find in His House the springs of a living faith. For such a man there can have been but one rallying-point for faithful Israelites—the Sanctuary of their God. But now the Ark was lost and the Sanctuary itself stood vacant and without significance. How then could the Presence of Jahweh be found there again? The difficulty might well appear to be insuperable, yet the

---

[1] 1 Sam. vii. 7 f.   [2] 1 Sam. xix. 18 f.

[3] Part at least of the present narrative of 1 Sam. i. seems to have been adapted from a story about Saul (cf. the play on the word 'asked'—in verse 20—which is the meaning of 'Saul', not of 'Samuel'). This, however, does not mean that the whole story is a fabrication.

facts themselves bear witness that it was overcome. By all the evidence of human conduct and experience, one of two consequences should have attended the disappearance of the Ark. Either Jahwism would have been entirely submerged by the Canaanite Baal-cultus or it would have survived as a purely prophetic, not as an institutional religion. In both events the ancient Sanctuary would have disappeared, its oracle would have been silenced, and its Priesthood permanently disbanded; and it must be regarded as extremely doubtful whether any people, at this early period, could have withstood for long the loss of these essentials of a national Faith. Instead of this, the institutional system of Jahwism remained unshaken upon its ancient bases, and the Sanctuary lost none of its old prestige. Transferred to Nob (at what date is uncertain) it continued to be served by a numerous priesthood, led by Ahitub the survivor of the Elidae, as the great religious centre of the tribes of Israel. Most significant fact of all, although no symbol of the Divine Presence had replaced the Ark,[1] the Presence (*Panim*) Bread was offered and renewed regularly as it must have been for centuries past.[2] To imagine that this distinctively Jahwistic custom could have been continued mechanically and in complete indifference to the catastrophe of the Ark's degradation is to lose sight of the living issues which were at stake in those critical years. Formalism is a type of decay with which every institutional religion is visited from time to time, but it is in periods of doctrinal security and internal peace that it makes its presence felt, not in those desperate moments

---

[1] The Ephod, whatever else it may have been, was certainly not an image, but served exclusively for oracular responses.

[2] 1 Sam. xxi. 1–9.

when the foundations of faith are shaken and the enemies of God are hammering at the gates. Then unreality, in whatever sphere it be found, shrivels into ashes under the blaze of imperious facts, and what emerges from those refining fires is not the dross of unintelligent make-believe, but the gold of a well-tried faith.

The preservation of an unshaken belief in Jahweh's Presence at His Sanctuary during those disastrous years which followed the capture of the Ark must be accounted, therefore, to be one of the most impressive features of Israelite history. Indeed it must be considered wholly inexplicable except on the assumption that through the influence of some great religious Leader a complete reorientation of religious thought took place. A new 'doctrine of the Divine Presence' must have been formulated which would exclude those very objects in which It had been once believed to centre, but which would yet embrace all else that had been cherished from the immemorial Past. Such a Leader, of course, existed already in Samuel, and it would be idle to look elsewhere; but it may well be doubted whether Samuel himself could have performed this miracle if he had not thrown his new teaching upon the background of the Exodus.

That he must, in fact, have done so, will become clearer with the investigation of the documents themselves. There are still traces in these of a doctrine of the Divine Presence which is in radical conflict with the more 'orthodox' and accepted view: and it is difficult, if not impossible, to attribute this to any other period except those years in which Samuel and the survivors of the old hereditary Priesthood were the joint-custodians of an Arkless shrine.[1]

[1] See below, p. 119.

5. The Priesthood of Gibeon

The story of Saul's repeated acts of disobedience and final rejection has long since become so familiar that it is difficult to realize that he was, in fact, an ardent, and even fanatical, Jahwist: yet this is patent, if only in those few documents relating to him which are uncoloured by Davidic prejudice. He appears almost from the first as one upon whom *"the spirit of Jahweh came mightily"*,[1] and this is confirmed by several evidences of his zeal. It was he who *"put away those that had familiar spirits, and the wizards"*,[2] and himself consulted the oracle of Jahweh which was for Israel the only lawful means of inquiry into the future.[3] It was he who in the flush of victory restrained his warriors from committing the sin of eating their spoil with the blood.[4] It was he who almost exterminated the Amalekites, the most bitter, as the most ancient, enemies of Jahweh's People.[5] It was he, finally, who *"in his zeal for . . . Israel"* put to the sword the non-Israelite (Hivite-Amorite) inhabitants of Gibeon and probably also of Beeroth.[6]

These facts must be borne in mind as indicating the strongly religious bent of Saul's policy; and they become of special importance in view of his ruthless massacre of the priests of Nob. Up to that tragic day Saul had shown no lack of confidence in Ahimelech the great-grandson of Eli,[7] and it was one of his own royal bodyguard whose presence at the sanctuary precipitated the disaster.[8] It

---

[1] 1 Sam. x. 6, 10.   [2] 1 Sam. xxviii. 3.
[3] 1 Sam. xiv. 18, where 'ephod' should be read for 'Ark': xxviii. 6.
[4] 1 Sam. xiv. 32 f.   [5] 1 Sam. xiv. 48.
[6] 2 Sam. xxi. 2. The assassins of Ishbosheth, Saul's son, were *"of Beeroth which is reckoned to Benjamin; and the Beerothites fled to Gittaim"* (2 Sam. iv. 3). The association is obvious.   [7] 1 Sam. xiv. 3 (Ahijah=Ahimelech).
[8] 1 Sam. xxi. 7; cf. 1 Sam. xxii. 17. (Driver, *Notes*, p. 176.)

is clear that Doeg accused the priest of having sought an oracle for David; an act which would be construed as high treason both against Jahweh and against His Anointed, and which Ahimelech himself deprecated with horror. It was enough. The man who had spared neither Hivites nor Amalekites was not likely to prove more merciful when the enemies were his own country-men, his own trusted friends. The sentence of death was pronounced, after the dreadful precedent of Achan,[1] on the whole unhappy village; but by whom it was executed remains uncertain.[2] Only one priest, Ahimelech's son Abiathar, escaped.

To our modern eyes, it was a mad and inexcusable outrage; yet it must be doubted if it would have appeared in that light at the time:[3] certainly for Saul himself there can have been no suggestion that the act was an ir-religious one; for to the end of his life he continued a devoted Jahwist.[4] This point must be emphasized, be-cause it is apt to be taken for granted that with the massacre of the priests of Nob the national Sanctuary itself ceased to exist. Such a conclusion would be wholly erroneous, for the quarrel of the King was not with his religion but with its official representatives. There is, in fact, no evidence at all that the Sanctuary was aban-doned; and we must assume, therefore, that it was trans-ferred elsewhere and that it was provided with a new priesthood.

---

[1] Joshua vii. 24–6.

[2] See below, p. 115. The strong anti-Saul colouring of the story makes its details suspect, in particular the suggestion that Doeg, single-handed, slaughtered a whole village must be received with extreme scepticism.

[3] Even the Judeans continued to support Saul against David; cf. 1 Sam. xxiii. 12; xxiv. 1; xxvi. 1 (all pro-David documents).

[4] 1 Sam. xxviii. 6.

(i) The *place* selected would seem to have been Gibeon, like Kirjath-jearim an Amorite (Hivite) fortress, but one from which its ancient inhabitants were driven by Saul. Here in later times was *"the great high place"*[1] where Solomon dreamed and offered sacrifice: here, according to the Chronicler, was the sanctuary of the Arkless Tabernacle which was committed by David to the care of Zadok, while Abiathar ministered to the Ark in Jerusalem:[2] here, finally, was the sacred hill, chosen by the Gibeonites themselves, where the sons of Saul were executed *"before Jahweh"*.[3] The combination of these three allusions may be held to amount to an almost definite proof. Whether or not a Tent had continued in existence from Mosaic times is open to doubt, though the description of a more solid building at Shiloh must not be urged against it.[4] There is at least one passage in which it is not merely assumed but required by Jahweh; and it is probable that the forces of puritan conservatism demanded it.[5] Be that as it may, the sanctuary which represented it might be intelligibly described as 'the Tabernacle' for which it stood, and it was this at which Ahimelech had ministered and which it was now Saul's duty to maintain in existence.

(ii) More important and very much less easily determined is the problem of the *new Priesthood* which he now installed. That it was the group or family from which Zadok sprang may be presumed without much hesita-

---

[1] 1 Kings iii. 4.　　　　　[2] 1 Chron. xvi. 39; 2 Chron. i. 3.

[3] 2 Sam. xxi. 6, 9. Driver, *Notes*, p. 351; Kittel, II, p. 131.

[4] 1 Sam. i. 9 (door-post); iii. 15 (doors of the house); iv. 18 (gate). But (*a*) these details may be anachronisms, (*b*) the Tent may have been pitched in a stone enclosure for safety.

[5] 2 Sam. vii. 1–7 (Nathan's warning). It is significant that David made no effort to build a house for the Ark, till he had asked permission.

tion, not merely on the evidence of the Chronicler already quoted, but much more because it is the most probable explanation of Zadok's equality of rank with Abiathar.[1] The restoration of the Ark necessarily involved the coexistence of the two great Sanctuaries, the one at Zion for the Tentless Ark itself, the other at Gibeon for the Arkless Tabernacle; and two Sanctuaries meant two chief-priests. The preference of Solomon for the Sanctuary at Gibeon will then explain the fact that it was Zadok, not Abiathar, who supported him in the struggle for the throne.

The chief difficulty, however, still remains to be solved, and it must be confessed that it can only be answered conjecturally. There are, then, certain reasons for believing that it was at this point that the Levites (as opposed to the ancient line of the Aaronids) came into possession of the official Jahweh-priesthood for the first time. This proposition will doubtless be disputed; but it may be pointed out in its favour that *before* this date there is no clear trace of the 'tribe' having served in this capacity, while by the end of the reign of Solomon the *failure* to appoint a Levitical priesthood to a Jahweh sanctuary was already accounted (by the Jerusalemites) a grievous sin.[2] It may be objected that the two 'Levite' stories appended to Judges are sufficient proof of the priestly character of the tribe from the earliest times: actually these tales are valueless as evidence. The need to establish the claims of Levi would naturally produce a stream of such pseudo-antiquarian literature and we

---

[1] 2 Sam. viii. 17; xv. 24–9.
[2] I Kings xii. 31 (Jeroboam). It should be noted also that the strong emphasis laid in Deuteronomy on the Levitical as the only lawful priesthood is a sign rather of its late date than of its high antiquity.

can no more trust these legends than we can accept the
adoption of Moses and later of Samuel into the tribe.[1]
Indeed we may have to recognize that the 'Aaronization'
of the Zadokites by their post-exilic descendants had
been preceded, long years before, by the 'Levitization'
of Aaron himself in the interests of these same Levite
Zadokites![2]

That the transfer of the Priesthood to the Levites took
place in the reign of Saul is unfortunately incapable of
verification. There is, however, one piece of evidence,
which, though indeterminate, may be briefly cited. The
so-called 'Blessing of Moses' (Deut. xxxiii), which in its
original form (it has certainly been interpolated) must
go back to pre-Davidic days,[3] connects very curiously the
tribes of Levi and Benjamin. That the composer was a
Levite may be inferred from the length of the blessing
pronounced upon this tribe, which is extolled for its
possession of the sacred Urim and Thummim and of the
duties of giving religious 'judgements' and offering sacrifice. It is, however, the blessing of Benjamin which is
the crux of the whole poem, and which can scarcely point
to any period in Israelite history but the reign of Saul:

"*The beloved of Jahweh shall dwell in safety by him;*
He covereth him all the day long,
And he dwelleth between his shoulders."[4]

Whatever the *exact* meaning of these enigmatic words
may be, it is clear that for some special reason the tribe
(or its representative) is 'beloved of Jahweh', Who is said,

[1] Exod. ii. 1 f.; 1 Chron. vi. 28.

[2] Exod. iv. 14 ("*Aaron thy brother the Levite*").

[3] *J.P.O.S.*, 1923, vol. iii, pp. 158 ff. (The date then assigned by the
present writer was to the end of the period of the Judges: the considerations offered above now require a slight advancement.)

[4] Deut. xxxiii. 12.

while protecting him, to dwell between his shoulders. Now at no time in history except in the reign of Saul could it have been said that the chief sanctuary of Jahweh lay within the borders of Benjamin. Shiloh was in the territory of Ephraim: Jerusalem was accounted, after its capture, to Judah.[1] Moreover, Judah in the blessing is lamented as temporarily separated from his brethren, a situation which may well have existed before Saul finally drove the Philistines from the mountains, but is incompatible with any later period, since no *Levite* could have written this of it from the reign of David onwards. The conjunction of this fact with the title 'Beloved of Jahweh' (the name which Solomon himself bore in after years) makes it very highly probable that the sanctuary referred to is Gibeon; the 'Beloved', Saul; and the period, that which followed his expulsion of the Philistines from the hill-country of Benjamin and marked his first efforts to extend his successes southwards.[2] Finally the fact that Levi is said to have obtained the priesthood by the test of 'Massah', in which he was regardless of the ties of kindred, will be seen to have a special significance when we examine the story related in Exodus.[3] A decisive judgement on the question is without doubt impossible, yet the cumulative force of the evidence is not to be ignored.

[1] Ps. lxxviii. 67–8. Bethel, which has been suggested, was in Ephraim (Joshua xvi. 1; xviii. 13): nor would any Levite have so written of his tribe in the anti-Levitical Northern Kingdom.

[2] The chronology of Saul's reign is hopelessly confused, but it must be remembered that it must have lasted between fifteen and twenty years and that for some period of it at least he was fighting more distant enemies than the Philistines (1 Sam. xiv. 47–8). The rout of the Philistines described in 1 Sam. xiv may well have enabled Benjamin to "*dwell in safety*", while Judah still remained in subjection.

[3] See below, p. 114.

6. The Priesthood of Jerusalem

It has been seen above that, with the establishment of the Ark in David's new capital, two separate priesthoods existed for a period side by side. With the accession of Solomon this anomalous state of affairs came to an abrupt end; for Abiathar, the last of the Elidae, had the misfortune to support the lawful but unsuccessful heir, Adonijah, and was banished in ignominy to his home village of Anathoth.[1] It is curious to reflect that it was a native of this same village (it may even have been a lineal descendant of the last Aaronid chief-priest) who in a later day pronounced the doom of both Ark and Temple and prophesied the coming of a new and better Covenant.[2] The removal of Abiathar left the Levite Zadokites in permanent and undisputed possession of the national Sanctuary; and there is reason to believe that their influence was now extended to embrace the whole of Israel. The precise allotment of 'Levitical cities', which we find now only in the 'priestly' sources,[3] must have had at one time (like the similar boundary registers)[4] a very real existence; for, indeed, the deliberate fabrication of such lists would be singularly pointless. But, if this is so, there is only one reign to which we can assign the careful selection of these cities; for there was only one reign in which both the organizing genius and the political power coincided. The friendship of Solomon with Zadok provided him, in fact, with one of the most potent weapons which the sovereign of a divided country can hope to wield against the forces of disrup-

[1] I Kings ii. 26–7.   [2] Jer. i. 1.
[3] Joshua xxi. 1–42; I Chron. vi. 57–81.
[4] Cf. *P.E.F.Q.S.*, 1929, pp. 228–41 (The Boundary of Ephraim and Manasseh).

tion: it gave him control of what was then the supreme unifying influence, the national Faith and the national memories of the Past. It can scarcely be doubted, therefore, that it was in these days that the scattered traditions of the elder and younger Priesthoods were first deliberately combined and partially reconciled: for, now and henceforward, the Ark and the Tabernacle were joined under a single hand, and the great Tradition could be built up into a semblance of coherent unity.[1]

[1] It will be evident (if the conclusions offered above are correct) that the Levites who were left in sole possession of the reunited Ark and 'Tabernacle' must have inherited two separate collections of material from which, with their own additions, they could construct a composite picture of the Past. One of these would have had its origin in the great high place of David's first capital, Hebron (2 Sam. v. 3; xv. 7–8), and would have been carried to the new Sanctuary at Zion by the Judean priests who were appointed to attend upon the Ark. The other would have been received by the Levites themselves, by way of the Sanctuaries of Gibeon and Nob, from Shiloh, i.e. from Northern Israel. Of these two sources, the Judean (J) and the Ephraimite (E), the second would naturally be the more favoured by the new Priesthood; and it is noteworthy that Deuteronomy, in which the special position of the Levites is repeatedly emphasized, follows E both in its historical narrative and in its Code. It is, in fact, difficult to resist the impression that the legislative nucleus of this book represents in substance 'an enlarged edition of the Book of the Covenant' (Exod. xx. 22–xxiii. 33 E), drawn up for use in the new Levitical cities (cf. Driver, *Deuteronomy*, p. x).

Chapter III

THE BASIS OF THE TRADITION

WITH the evidences of Israelite history fresh in our minds, it may be wiser to leave aside for the moment the earlier incidents of the Exodus, and to proceed at once to the point at which the confusion of documentary structure is most conspicuous, namely, the scene of the Theophany at the Mount of God, and its sequel. When the various 'courses' of this part of the narrative have been as far as possible dated and interpreted, the remainder of the story will present less difficulty.

I

To construct out of the materials which are to be found scattered up and down the present Book of Exodus a coherent and simple account of the events at Horeb,[1] is in itself a task of no great difficulty. Very fortunately we already have such an account in the opening chapters of Deuteronomy, which is regarded to-day as being based on a single and comparatively early source (E).[2] It is only necessary, then, in building up our picture to confine ourselves to such details as are identical in both books, outstepping these limits only where logic demands it.

The story may be said to open with the appearance of a Pillar of Cloud and Fire which meets the Israelites at the Red Sea and leads them by day and night to the

[1] On the alternative, and now more familiar, name *Sinai* see below, p. 131.

[2] A. C. Welch, *Deuteronomy, The Framework of the Code*, 1932, p. 7.

Mount of God.[1] There from the burning summit of the Mount Jahweh utters the Ten Words, which He then delivers to Moses written upon two Tables of Stone; Tables, be it noted, both made and inscribed by Himself.[2] With these most sacred objects in his hands, Moses prepares to return in triumph to his people, but the sight of the idolatrous worship of the Golden Calf overwhelms him with terrible anger. He dashes the Sacred Tables to the earth, and they are smashed in pieces.[3] Yet this disaster is not irremediable. The Tables are replaced, at God's command, by others, hewn and (apparently) written by Moses himself but bearing the same contents.[4] Although but a man-made substitute for the first, these new Memorials are to be regarded as equally sacred. A special receptacle must be provided for them, since they are to accompany Israel on its departure from the Mount and externalize the continual Presence (Panim) of Jahweh in its midst.[5] An Ark or chest of acacia wood is, therefore, made to receive them and a special Tent is furnished as a movable Sanctuary.[6] Thus equipped, the people set forward at last from Horeb, the Ark moving on before them and selecting a resting-place at the end of each stage of the journey.[7]

The story, thus presented in broadest outline, is certainly straightforward and consistent; yet, even as it

[1] Exod. xiii. 21: Deut. i. 33.
[2] Exod. xxiv. 12; xxxii. 15; Deut. iv. 11–13; v. 22.
[3] Exod. xxxii. 15–20; Deut. ix. 15–21.
[4] Exod. xxxiv. 1–4, 28; Deut. x. 1–4.
[5] Exod. xxxii. 34; xxxiii. 14: Deut. x. 11.
[6] Deut. x. 1–5 (Ark). Both the Ark and the Tent must have been mentioned in the earlier documents of Exodus: their place has been filled by the long descriptions of the 'priestly' school. On Exod. xxxiii. 7 f. see below, p. 115.
[7] Num. x. 33.

stands, it contains at least two features which cannot be accepted without a much closer examination:

1. THE CHARACTER OF THE TABLES OF STONE

It was pointed out in the previous chapter[1] that, while the core of the Tradition seemed to identify the contents of the Ark with two mysterious fragments of stone, it by no means followed that the *description* of these could be relied upon. We have now to face this difficulty. It has been widely recognized by scholars that the peculiar sanctity of the Ark, and the supernatural powers which were ascribed to it, above all its strange semi-identification with Jahweh Himself, are by no means satisfactorily explained, if we are to assume that the current tradition is true. It is, in fact, almost inconceivable that any people in a comparatively low stage of cultural development should attach a Divine Power and Presence to two stones which contained no more than a series of legal injunctions written by their Leader. If against this it be argued that the second pair of Tables was equally written by God Himself according to one version of the story,[2] it must be replied that even on this supposition the matter remains unaccountable. 'Tablets of the Law do not imply the presence of the Lawgiver':[3] it must, moreover, be taken as certain that if these Tables bore the Ten Words, they must have been inscribed by a human hand in human characters; and if this was so, the chief difficulty remains unaltered. The gravity of this problem is reflected in the remarkable diversity of theories which have been proposed for its solution;[4] such a diversity, indeed, as to make it appear insoluble. Yet, if the clue

---

[1] See above, p. 85.

[2] Deut. x. 2–4; cf. Exod. xxxiv. 1 as against Exod. xxxiv. 28.

[3] Benzinger (McNeile, p. 162).   [4] For references see above, p. 84, n. 1.

which we already hold is a sound one, it should be strong enough to find a way through the tangle.

Let it be assumed, then, that the original stones (whatever they were) were destroyed by the Philistines. This fact must, of course, have been an open secret to many, when David resolved to rehabilitate the Ark. If, therefore, it was to resume its sacred function as the representative of the Divine Presence, some modification of the old tradition became imperative. Could it be, after all, that it was *the Ark itself*, rather than its contents, around which the supernatural Power was focused? Clearly this must be so, since had it been otherwise its contents could never have suffered destruction. (Here we see the relevance of these stories about the Ark's death-dealing powers in Philistia, at Beth-shemesh, and at Perez-uzzah.) But, if this were so, what had these contents been? That, according to the hitherto accepted tradition, they were stones, if not inscribed by Jahweh, at any rate His handiwork, is an inference based upon their later historical substitutes which may be as near the truth as it is possible to attain:[1] but since this belief had become untenable, *ex hypothesi*, with their destruction, an alternative explanation must be supplied. In other words, while it was still necessary to acknowledge that the Ark had contained *something* before its capture—for since it was obviously designed to be a receptacle, it could hardly be thought of as having been empty from the first—an effort must be made to show that the loss of these contents, serious as it was, was not of the gravity that had been supposed. *It must, in short, be suggested that the stones which the Ark contained, when captured, were not after all the gift and*

[1] See below, p. 149 f. The first tables were "*the work of God and the writing was the writing of God, graven upon the tables*". Exod. xxxii. 16.

the handiwork of Jahweh Himself, but that they were substitutes hewn and written by Moses in consequence of some disaster in which the first Stones were destroyed. That even these substitute Tables possessed a peculiar sanctity could not, of course, be denied; but it could be argued that they possessed this not in their own right but because the Ten Words, which were (now) believed to have been written on them, *had first been pronounced by Jahweh Himself.*[1] Once this new tradition had become sufficiently established, the brilliant victories of David, under the leadership of the Ark, must inevitably have submerged the old humiliating memory of its degradation, so that it became gradually a widely accepted belief that its contents had not after all been lost, but were veritably those Tables of Stone which Moses had brought down with him the second time from the Mount.

If this explanation appears to be as involved as it is conjectural, some allowance must at least be made for an attempt to face a real and complicated difficulty, which it is certainly much more easy to ignore. It can at least be contended in its favour that it deals not merely with a serious historical lacuna but also with an equally serious documentary problem: it accounts, in a word, for one of the most extraordinary episodes in the present Book of Exodus:

2. The Golden Calf[2] and the Breaking and Renewal of the Tables (Exod. xxxii. 1–xxxiii. 6; xxxiv. 1–28).

The story of the Golden Calf carries on its face a reasonably obvious hint of its date. That there is an

---

[1] Cf. Deut. v. 22. See below, Additional Note on the 'Divine Presence', p. 133 f.

[2] We may preserve the familiar title, though, strictly speaking, the animal was doubtless a young bull. (Wainwright, *P.E.F.Q.S.*, 1934, p. 37.)

intimate connexion between this episode and the historical establishment of Calf-worship by Jeroboam I admits
of no doubt, nor is it less certain which of them precedes
the other in point of time. The words "*These be thy gods*",
&c., as used by Jeroboam (with plural verbs) are no more
than apposite where the two calves at Bethel and Dan
are in question, but the same phrase (with the same plural
verbs) as used by Aaron for a single image is not only
unnatural but meaningless. But we can go farther. The
awkward attribution of these identical words to Aaron
must then be deliberate. The writer must have *intended*
an attack upon Jeroboam, and the most obvious conclusion is that this attack was contemporary. The question, then, arises whether the same can be said not merely
of this single phrase but of the whole episode of the
Golden Calf. It will be seen below that this episode
has been grafted upon a different and earlier story in
which Aaron already figured as responsible for a national
backsliding. The story of the Calf is, therefore, certainly
not original in its present form, and there are other
reasons for believing that it formed no part of the earliest
traditions. It is strange, for example, that Elijah appears
to have raised no protest against the Calf-worship of the
Northern Kingdom. If the sin of the Golden Calf had
been known to him, the glaring resemblance to it of the
worship of Dan and Bethel could hardly have failed to
excite his deepest anger. But more strange even than
Elijah's silence is that of Hosea, who inveighs particularly
against the Calf-worship of his contemporaries.[1] Not
only does he make no reference to the Golden Calf but he
regards the whole of Israel's desert-wanderings as a
period of unalloyed innocence and happiness, and the

---

[1] Hos. viii. 5–6; xiii. 2.

first breach of loyalty to Jahweh which he records is the downfall of Israel at Baal-peor.[1] The most obvious conclusion from these facts is that the story was unknown to the northern tribes, that it was in fact composed in the environment of the Temple at Jerusalem, and that it marked a deliberate attempt to denounce Jeroboam's idolatrous innovation by transforming an already existing account of some sin committed at Horeb into an exact replica of this new apostasy. It may be claimed, finally, that this attack must have been launched almost immediately after the installation of the Calves, for no other moment is psychologically so probable. The mere lapse of time will always blunt the edge of anger or hostility, and when the Calves became familiar objects of worship, the incitement to denounce them would wane in power as the prospect of a successful issue also faded. It appears, therefore, reasonable to date the whole of this episode (so far as it concerns the Calf) to the years immediately following the Sin of Jeroboam.

It has been said that behind the episode of the Golden Calf lie the remains of an earlier story which has been almost entirely erased to make room for it. It was in this that Aaron first appeared as responsible for a grave offence committed by Israel at Horeb.[2] The nature of this offence is indicated by the reference to the Jahweh-feast in verse 5, the revelry in verse 6, and the statement in verse 25 that "*the people were broken loose; for Aaron had let them loose for a whispering among their enemies*". The Septuagint perhaps preserves a further trace of this trans-

---

[1] Hos. ix. 10. See above, p. 26.

[2] Procksch, p. 90 f. The view held by some scholars that the Calf-worship of Bethel was in some way associated with Aaron through his descendants seems, on this analysis, to have little in its favour.

gression, for in verse 18 it replaces *the noise of singing* by 'the noise of those who begin (to be drunken with) wine' (ἐξαρχόντων οἴνου). These scattered hints are sufficiently clear to show their incongruity with the story of the Golden Calf. *That* sin consists in the worship of a graven image designed to take the place of the God of Moses as the leader of Israel to the land of Canaan; *this* in the holding of a Jahweh-feast which is allowed to degenerate into an orgy of unbridled licence.

Is this episode, in its turn, a part of the original Tradition? Once more the silence of Hosea seems to condemn it. It has, in fact, been suggested that the major portion of the incident (with the appointment of the Levitical Priesthood which would in that case have been its *raison d'être*) has been transferred to this context from an original association with Baal-peor.[1] If this were so, however, the mention of *Aaron* would have to be treated as a later and somewhat meaningless addition, since his death, whether at Moserah or Mount Hor, is said to have taken place some considerable time before Israel's arrival at Shittim. A more satisfactory explanation may be arrived at, if it is realized that the importance of the story lies not in itself at all, but in *the fact that it provides an explanation for the destruction of the first Tables*. Here is indeed the crucial point of the whole problem, for it is precisely this episode which is the object of the gravest suspicion. The doubts which it excites are, in part, of its own making. The initial question, in fact, is not whether such an incident really happened at Horeb but whether, had it happened, it would have been recorded so strangely in the ancient Tradition, even if (which is more than doubtful) it had been recorded at all. Taken as it stands,

[1] Gressmann, *Mose*, p. 209.

the action of Moses is incomprehensibly rash and violent; doubly so, indeed, if he had already been warned what to expect.[1] However great the sin of his people, nothing could surely justify his deliberate destruction of these Sacred Tables which had but that moment been placed so solemnly in his hands. Yet the narrator ignores this difficulty entirely, nor does he suggest that this action either merited or received any expression of displeasure from Jahweh. He merely relates that new Tables had to be hewn by Moses; and, even so, he does not explain how they could be substitutes for the Divine Handiwork of the first, for he leaves it in doubt whether it was Jahweh or Moses who wrote upon them.

But if the internal evidence of this scene is a strong argument against its historical value, critical analysis reveals an even more obvious flaw. It can scarcely be doubted that in the earlier documentary sources the Voice which Israel heard speaking with Moses out of the Mount was thought of as intelligible to him alone, while to the People it was no more than a sound of supernatural and terrifying thunder.[2] Its whole purpose, in fact, was to declare Jahweh's peculiar intimacy with His servant and to be an outward guarantee of the revelation which he was to receive. But if there was originally no suggestion of the Ten Words having been proclaimed aloud from the thick darkness, the Divine potency with which this Utterance invested them likewise disappears, and with it the special sanctity of the Tables with which they are so closely associated.[3] Here we encounter con-

---

[1] Exod. xxxii. 7–14; Deut. ix. 12.

[2] Exod. xix. 19: "*Moses spake and God answered* HIM *by a voice.*" The narrative is continued in xx. 18 f., where the people beg that Moses, not God, shall speak with them. Cf. McNeile, p. 113.

[3] See above, p. 108, and Deut. v. 22, where the fact of Jahweh

fessedly an insuperable obstacle, for the interpolation of this new view of the Theophany has necessarily erased all traces of the original nature of the Stones:[1] yet the fact that this is so must not be allowed to blind us to the definitive conclusions of criticism.

On all counts, then, it is impossible to regard this episode as having formed part of the original Tradition. It is a massive fragment of superstructure built, it is true, upon the memory of the sacred contents of the Ark, but having a definite purpose of its own. What that purpose was, we are now in a position to realize. *It was to minimize the gravity of the Ark's capture and of the loss of the Stones within it.*[2] That the description of the causes of this disaster followed deliberately the historical facts of the actual calamity may be conjectured, though it is not immediately obvious. The indirect reason for the catastrophe at Aphek is given by the writer in Samuel as the abuse of their priestly office by the sons of Eli, the Aaronid:[3] while in the Mosaic narrative the sin is in the first place that of Aaron himself in allowing a Jahweh-feast to degenerate into a drunken orgy. Here indeed the parallel is a loose one, but there may have been other views on the question which brought the two stories into a closer affinity. The sins of these young men, however grave in themselves, were purely personal, and afford very insufficient reasons for a punishment which involved the entire Nation:[4] on

uttering the Words AND NO MORE is combined with His writing them on the Tables.

[1] It may be suggested, as a conjecture, that they bore mysterious 'characters' suggesting the Divine Name JHWH. See below, p. 149 f.

[2] See above, p. 107.

[3] 1 Sam. ii. 12–17, 22–36.

[4] It should be remembered that the writer of 1 Sam. ii. is concerned rather with the history of Samuel and the Elidae than with the national disaster itself.

I

the other hand, we are not without evidence that the annual Jahweh-feast at Shiloh had been allowed, prior to the capture of the Ark, to fall very far short of its ideal of innocent happiness. The rape of the Shilonite maidens *"who came out to dance in the dances"*[1] is a disagreeable reminder of the degree of licence into which the old vintage festivals could be allowed to fall; and it is certain that such orgies would not have passed unchallenged. There was never wanting in Israel a strong puritanical element, led (at least in later times) by the Rechabites, which viewed with detestation practices at once repulsive and grossly unloyal to Jahweh: and there must have been many others less extreme in their views who, in looking back at the awful tragedy of the Ark's capture, read it as a Divine punishment on a nation which had been allowed by its own Priesthood to become *"a whispering among its enemies"*.

There remains, in conclusion, the story of the consecration of the Levites to the Priesthood, to which allusion has already been made.[2] We are told that on seeing how Aaron had *"let the people loose"*, Moses stood at the camp's gate and cried: *"Whoso is on Jahweh's side, to me!"* His call was answered by *"all the sons of Levi"*, who in obedience to his command drove their way through the camp from gate to gate, *"slaying every man his brother and every man his companion and every man his neighbour"*. As a reward for this refusal to regard the closest ties of kin or kind, the Levites were consecrated to the priesthood. A memory of this act of heroic mercilessness seems to survive in the 'Blessing of Moses' upon this 'tribe', as explaining its enjoyment

---

[1] Judges xxi. 19 f.
[2] Exod. xxxii. 26–9 (as an explanation of the 'testing' at Massah). Cf. Deut. x. 8.

of its sacred office. In Deuteronomy, on the other hand, the same statement appears not in direct association with the disgrace of Aaron (for whom Moses is here said to intercede), but as a sequel to the writing of the Sacred Tables and the making of the Ark. Possibly its connexion with the disaster caused by Aaron's weakness was not at first a very close one; indeed, as has been said, the whole episode is regarded by some scholars as having been transferred to this context from Baal-peor.[1]

If, however, we accept the suggestion which has been advanced in the previous chapter, the explanation becomes clear. There is only one known historical occasion on which the Priesthood of Israel changed hands, and that was as the result of the alleged treachery of the priests of Nob. The leader of these priests was the surviving descendant of the Aaronids; and the curse which followed him was the curse pronounced upon Eli. Though the connexion of the Levites' appointment to the Priesthood was thus only indirectly with the disaster of Aphek, it was by no means void of all association with it. May it not also have been the new priests themselves who executed the ruthless sentence on their own 'brothers'? We are apt to think of the Levites as a meek and downtrodden class; but the earlier references to them (such as this) give them a very different character;[2] and we can hardly suppose that they would have been chosen to escort the Ark, if they had not been among the most fanatical champions of Jahweh.

II

So far, for all their complexity, the documents which have been examined have followed the familiar and

---

[1] See above, p. 111. [2] Cf. Gen. xlix. 5.

'historic' conception of the Divine Presence as in some way associated with the Ark and its Contents. Now, however, a series of passages is to be studied in which an entirely different view makes its appearance. The first, and most important, of these is embedded in the present narrative between the destruction of the first Tables and the making of their substitutes, a position which is all the more significant because the passage itself has no kind of connexion with either of these.[1] It relates that it was the custom of Moses to pitch 'the' Tent (which he called the Tent of Meeting) outside the Camp, where it could be sought by all who desired directions from Jahweh. As to what precise reason for 'inquiring of Jahweh' the people had at this early stage, we are not informed; nor, very clearly, is this the immediate concern of the narrator. His object in describing the custom is rather to inform his readers that when *Moses himself* went out to the Tent, a special supernatural phenomenon immediately followed. It was *then* that the Pillar of Cloud descended and stood at the door of the Tent (after Moses had entered it), and it was from the midst of this Pillar, visible in His own form to His servant only, that Jahweh *"spake unto Moses face to face as a man speaketh to his friend"*. From the associated passage in Num. xii (the punishment of Miriam) we learn that this phenomenon of the Pillar of Cloud was not one which remained permanently over, or at the door of, the Tent. It descended for special purposes and then departed. Nor did the Presence within it enter the Tent,[2] which served, according to this view, as

[1] Exod. xxxiii. 7–11.

[2] Gressmann (*Mose*, p. 244) is in error in describing the Pillar 'Gleich einem Gespann, das draussen wartet'. There is no suggestion of Jahweh's leaving the Pillar and entering the Tent, for those already within it must come out to face Him.

a kind of protecting enclosure from whose shelter men might converse with God without fear of instant destruction. It is thus conceived as fulfilling the same purpose as the cave or cleft in the rock out of which Moses was permitted to behold the Divine Form;[1] and not only Moses himself, but also on one occasion both Aaron and Miriam were able in this way to speak with Jahweh and live. It should, however, be noticed that even in this tradition there are signs of confusion or misunderstanding. In the description of the 'inspiration' of the seventy elders in Num. xi. 23 f. the men are described as being posted *"round about the Tent"* which certainly suggests that they were all outside it. A further difficulty arises over the precise part which was supposed to have been played by Joshua.[2] The presence in the Tent of this youthful minister who never departed out of it naturally recalls the familiar story of the young Samuel. But the duties of Samuel were clearly connected with the Ark of God and, amongst other matters, with the superintendence of the lamp of God which burned before it.[3] The Tent or 'Temple' in which he worked and slept was, in short, a place which owed its whole sanctity to the Divine Palladium. There the Presence of Jahweh dwelt in the midst of Israel, and the house which sheltered It must be watched over day and night. When we turn back to the Tent in which Joshua is said to have ministered, the entire situation is seen at once to be different. Not only is there no Ark in it but the Presence of Jahweh remains Itself outside. The minister is there, but where is the need of his ministry?

---

[1] Exod. xxxiii. 22. Morgenstern (*The Oldest Document of the Hexateuch*, 1927, p. 38 f.) rightly compares the vigil of Elijah with this function of the Tent of Meeting.   [2] Exod. xxxiii. 11.   [3] 1 Sam. iii. 3.

It may be thought that the divergence between these two traditions is less real than apparent and that they can be reconciled on the explicit assumptions of the narrative. Since, *ex hypothesi*, the second Tables of Stone have still to be brought down from the Mount and the Ark is not yet sanctified by their presence, it might be possible to regard the appearance of Jahweh in the 'Pillar of Cloud' as a purely temporary Presence vouchsafed only until the first Tables have been replaced. This view is, however, untenable for several reasons. Firstly, it takes no account of the wholly different purpose to which the Tent is put; secondly, it leaves unexplained the presence and duties of Joshua; finally, it is vitiated by the mention of other similar appearances of the Cloud *after* the people have taken their departure from Horeb. Two of these, the 'inspiration' of the seventy elders and the punishment of Miriam, have already been mentioned. In neither passage is there any suggestion of a Presence within the Tent and in the second of them it seems to be entirely excluded. But, apart from these, we have to reckon with what seems to be a development of the 'Pillar' tradition which regards the Cloud as having been the visible sign of Jahweh's guiding Presence from the Mount of God onwards.[1] As the *Ark* is elsewhere said to have performed this function,[2] the contradiction would appear to be complete, and any kind of reconciliation becomes impossible. It is true that the 'priestly' writers had their own explanation to offer. From Sinai onwards, according to their view, the Divine Glory dwelt above the Mercy Seat of the Ark in the Cloud which filled the most Holy Place and covered the Tabernacle, but when the people were to set forward on the next stage of their journey, the Cloud

[1] Num. xiv. 14.   [2] Num. x. 33.

removed from the Tabernacle and went before them.[1]
That is undoubtedly an adroit attempt at a solution, but
it succeeds in evading rather than in reconciling the
difficulties; and it is certainly not one with which modern
scholarship can remain satisfied.

Here once more, in short, as in the primary problem
which concerns the Ark, we find ourselves beset with a
whole series of baffling and apparently insoluble contradictions. That they are due to the amalgamation of in-
harmonious traditions derived from a variety of sources
is a conclusion which critical analysis has long since
established, but here all agreement ceases. Whether the
Ark (with or without the Tables) belongs to the primary
stratum of the original deposit and the Tent and the
Pillar of Cloud to a secondary source, or whether, indeed,
these values ought not to be completely reversed is a
problem which has been long and warmly debated.[2]

Once more it may not be altogether presumptuous to
claim that we hold the clue to this enigma, for our review
of the critical years which followed the capture of the Ark
has led us to expect precisely this divergence from the
'historic' doctrine of the Presence.[3] This passage, which
has been so significantly inserted between the destruction
and renewal of the Tables, betrays in every line the purpose for which it was originally composed. It was designed to create faith in an *unseen* Presence of Jahweh at
a Sanctuary from which the Ark had vanished. The
puzzling figure of the young Joshua ministering in an
empty Tent is simply a reflection of the youthful Samuel

[1] Exod. xi. 36–8; Num. ix. 15–23. See below, p. 134.

[2] Cf. Kittel, p. 317; Sellin, 'Das Zelt Jahwes' in *Alttest. Stud.*, 1913,
p. 168 f. Among others Baentsch and Procksch uphold the first of these
views, Westphal the second.

[3] See above, p. 95.

himself ministering before the Ark at Shiloh. For a little
reflection will show that these two must overlap. It must
be maintained that even though the Ark was at Shiloh
when Samuel first came there as a child, it was not for the
Ark's sake, but for the unseen Presence of Jahweh that
he tended the lamp of God within the Sanctuary. Even,
then, when the Ark had departed—it would be thought,
for ever—that Presence would still remain; and the people
might still go to consult the oracle, to offer their sacrifices,
in a word, to 'meet' their God, as they used to go *"without
the Camp"* when Israel walked through the Wilderness.

But here a very natural question could hardly fail to
be raised: 'Since that Presence was without any visible
symbol like the Ark, what guarantee had the people that
It was really there?' To this the answer was that the
Sanctuary had been consecrated for all time as the
Nation's 'Tent of Meeting' by the fact that when Jahweh
spoke with Moses a visible Appearance was granted
which all Israel might behold and worship from their
own tent doors:

*"The Pillar of Cloud descended and stood at the door of the
    Tent . . .*
And Jahweh spake unto Moses face to face
As a man speaketh unto his friend."[1]

If, on this, it were asked further 'Why should not that
Appearance be vouchsafed *now*? Why was it not granted,
for example, to Samuel himself, who was blessed with
"vision" beyond all other prophets?'[2] the answer (Num.
xii. 1–15) must be, in effect, a stern rebuke of such presumptuous imaginings. When even Aaron and Miriam
claimed this right, as being equal in prophetic gifts to

---

[1] Exod. xxxiii. 10–11.   [2] 1 Sam. iii. 1, 21.

Moses himself, they did indeed speak with Jahweh in the Pillar of Cloud at the door of the Tent, but Miriam departed from it a leper *"as white as snow"*. Once more the lesson is driven home that what happened at Horeb when Moses spoke with God can never be expected to happen on this earth again:

"My servant Moses is not so [as any other prophets, however gifted] . . . *with him I will speak mouth to mouth, even manifestly . . . and the form of Jahweh shall he behold."*

The repeated emphasis on the appearance of the Presence for Moses *and for him only*, with the implied warning to expect no such manifestation hereafter when he is no longer on earth to witness it (for Presence and Pillar are of course inseparable) receives its full significance only when it is placed in the context of a later day and seen as an essential element in the teaching of Samuel.[1] By stories such as these,[2] based upon the age-long tradition of the Pillar of Cloud and Fire, a new consciousness of God's unseen Presence at His Sanctuary must have been created and fortified, while the thoughts of Israelite patriots were directed back to those great days in the past, when Jahweh delivered His people by signs and wonders and spoke to Moses out of the thick darkness and the Cloud. Best of all, the despair which followed upon

[1] Such teaching would have been meaningless at any other period of Israelite history, since from the installation of the Ark in Solomon's Temple the doctrine of the Presence resumed its original form, the 'focus' being once more externalized within the 'Tent'.

[2] The story of Eldad and Medad (Num. xi. 24–9) belongs clearly to this cycle. It deals with the problem of 'unauthorized' prophets and recalls the saying *"Is Saul also among the prophets?"* (1 Sam. x. 11, 12). The enigmatical question *"And who is their* (LXX *his*) *father?"* may perhaps be explained as an indignant protest from the 'professional' prophets. If this is so, the noble rebuke put into the mouth of Moses (Num. xi. 29) may well have been heard from the lips of Samuel himself.

the loss of the Ark and its Sacred Stones was swept away as the tide of faith rolled back. Holy as these were, they were seen to be no longer essential to faith or worship. Once more the Holy Bread could be spread before the Presence, and the Divine Counsel sought; and as each sacrifice smoked up to Heaven, the pillar of its cloud and fire at the door of the Sanctuary brought back to the mind the glory and graciousness of the God of Moses. Jahweh Sebaoth would yet again deliver His People.

The details of the foregoing reconstruction are wholly imaginative, and it need hardly be said that the reader must accept or reject them as he will. It is to be hoped, however, that the slowly accumulating weight of the aetiological evidence will by this time have convinced him that the main lines of the argument are sound. However they may be explained, the documents which have just been studied can in no sense claim to be historical records: they are 'Sacred Stories' composed for the inculcation of a particular Truth; parables of no small spiritual value, but not authentic memories of a great Past. Nor is their relative position in the superstructure more doubtful. Though earlier in date than the passages which deal with the Tables of Stone, they are at a greater remove from the primal base of the Tradition: for the facts on which they are founded—the Tent and the Pillar of Cloud—while of necessity present, are formed into a combination which is essentially unreal.

III

An attempt may now be made to secure a closer view of the groundwork of this extraordinary Tradition; for such difficulties as still remain are a great deal less formidable and may be dealt with as they are encountered. The story opens[1] with the flight of Moses to Midian, that region of the present northern Hejaz which lies to the east of the Gulf of Akaba and the mountains of ancient Edom.[2] Here, while one day keeping the flocks of his father-in-law the priest of Midian, he found himself in the vicinity of the mysterious Mount of God. Then followed the apparition of the Burning Bush and the Call which sent him back to Egypt as the herald and instrument of Jahweh's deliverance. Of his effort to convince and convert his People, practically no trace remains:[3] we are conducted almost immediately to that succession of devastating blows which humbled the pride of Pharaoh and encouraged Israel to escape. (That the 'plagues' were needed as much for the second purpose as for the first has already been suggested[4]: the fact of Pharaoh's pursuit reveals an enemy neither overawed nor rendered utterly impotent.) Disentangled from later additions and embellishments, the course of events can be followed without great difficulty,[5] and the stupefying effects of its familiarity can be best avoided if it is described in modern terms.

Some time after the return of Moses from Midian the waters of the Nile suddenly turned blood-red, the fish in the river died, and the river itself stank.[6] This was, however, only the beginning of evils; for the innumerable

---

[1] It is unnecessary here to deal with the birth-story of Moses, which is very clearly based on a familiar group of legends (Gressmann, *Mose*, p. 7 f.).   [2] See below, Appendix II.
[3] See above, p. 50.   [4] See above, p. 49.
[5] For analysis see Driver and McNeile, *ad loc.*, and Gressmann, *Mose*, pp. 66–7. A comparison of these will show that it is virtually impossible to distinguish the two older sources in any but the broadest features.
[6] Exod. vii. 20–1.

frogs, which normally live out their lives among the reeds, were driven ashore by this pollution of the waters, swarmed over all the fields and into all the houses, and then died in their myriads. "*They gathered them together in heaps; and the land stank.*"[1] From these masses of corruption a plague of poisonous flies inevitably followed; and these spread the infection first among animals and then among human beings.[2] Then two further blows fell: appalling hailstorms smote down the rising crops and a host of locusts completed the devastation.[3] Finally, as a kind of awful climax, a "*darkness that could be felt*" descended upon the whole land, so that "*they saw not one another, neither rose any from his place for three days*".[4] It was then that Moses seized the opportunity to extricate his people from Egypt and to hurry them across the wilderness to the safety of the Land of Midian. The route he is said to have taken is described with curious care, as if it had long been a mystery to the Israelites that he should have chosen it. It was not the western coast-road to the "*land of the Philistines*": it was "*the way of the wilderness of the Yam Suph*", which, as we know from other passages, was the Gulf of Akaba.[5] It was then that the crowning miracle occurred. As the fugitives approached in desperation the southern extremity of the great frontier wall (there is a suggestion in the narrative that they had already attempted to pass through it farther to the north and had been foiled),[6] the arm of the sea which should have blocked their passage retreated suddenly and left the foreshore dry.[7] Then followed one of the most

---

[1] Exod. viii. 13–14.   [2] Exod. viii. 24; ix. 6; xii. 29.
[3] Exod. ix. 25; x. 13–15.   [4] Exod. x. 23.
[5] Exod. xiii. 17–18; cf. 1 Kings ix. 26; Num. xiv. 25, xxi. 4; Deut. i. 40.   [6] Exod. xiii. 18; cf. xiv. i (P).
[7] Exod. xiv. 21.

dramatic scenes in history, the never-to-be-forgotten night of Israel's passage, and the dawn which saw the chariots of Egypt swept to destruction by the rage of returning waters.[1]

And now, in the safety of the desert, a new miracle was performed:[2] a colossal Pillar of Cloud made its appearance which guided the people unerringly to the Mount of God. This Pillar which led them on, in cloud by day, in fire by night, left behind it an ineffaceable memory. No feature indeed of that amazing journey impressed itself with greater force upon the imagination of Israel. It was said to have been foretold to Moses by Jahweh as the sign that His People would seek Him at His Holy Mountain:[3] it was thought to have been present even at the crossing of the Red Sea as a barrier between the fugitives and their enemy:[4] it became for a while the symbol which replaced the Ark, as the leader of Israel from Horeb onwards[5] and as the 'focus' of the Divine Presence at the door of the Tent: and, finally, at the hands of the priestly writers, it entered the Tent itself and penetrated even into the Holy of Holies, as the mysterious veil of cloud and thick darkness which shrouded the ineffable Glory.[6] All this should be borne in mind when we attempt to interpret this phenomenon; for it is not wise to dismiss with an empty rationalization a memory so potent and so enduring.

The journey from the Red Sea to Horeb must be treated, as far as the Tradition is concerned, as a com-

---

[1] Exod. xiv. 30–1.   [2] Exod. xiii. 21; Neh. ix. 19.

[3] Exod. iii. 12. (This is the most probable significance of the 'token'.)

[4] Exod. xiv. 19. (The earlier statement was that it *"departed not from before the people"*.)

[5] Num. x. 34 (Deut. i. 33?); Exod. xl. 36 (P): Num. ix. 17 (P).

[6] I Kings viii. 10; Ezek. x. 3 f. See below, p. 134.

plete blank. The itinerary given, where it is not obviously aetiological as in the episode of Mara (Bitter) and Elim (Palms),[1] must be assigned to the antiquarian researches of a much later age, most probably when the scene of the Theophany had been located in the granite mountains of the Sinai Peninsula.[2] The battle with Amalek at Rephidim[3] is certainly misplaced in its present context, not merely because Moses is represented as enfeebled by age and Joshua as having assumed the command of the army, but because the water-miracle which immediately precedes it places the Israelites already in the vicinity of the Midianite Horeb, and therefore beyond the reach of the Amalekites. It is possible that this bitter memory belonged to a later period in the Wanderings, when Israel made its abortive effort against the cities of the Negeb and was driven back in confusion into the Arabah.[4]

The arrival at the Mount of God was the signal for an event of appalling and mysterious grandeur, some details of which can still be gathered from the documents:

> "*On the third day, when it was morning, there were thunders and lightnings, and a thick cloud upon the mount, and the voice of a trumpet exceeding loud; and all the people that were in the camp trembled. And Moses brought forth the people out of the camp to meet God; and they stood at the nether part of the mount. And [the] mount . . . was altogether on smoke . . . and the smoke thereof ascended as the smoke of a furnace, and the whole mount quaked greatly. And when the voice of the*

---

[1] Elim may have been identified with the present port of Tor (Gk. Phoinikon, i.e. 'Palms'): the neighbouring tribes were called Maranitae. Kittel, I, p. 325.

[2] See below, Additional Note on Horeb-Sinai.

[3] Exod. xvii. 8–16.   [4] Num. xiv. 45 (cf. Deut. xxv. 17).

trumpet waxed louder and louder, Moses spake, and God answered him by a voice."[1]

With this tremendous sign of the Divine favour to seal and establish his authority, Moses ascended the Mount and *"drew near unto the thick darkness where God was"*. From this point onwards the original narrative has been erased to give place to the Book of the Covenant (E), the priestly description of the Ark and its equipment, and the story of the breaking of the Tables. It must, however, have related how Moses brought back the Sacred Stones and placed them in the Ark which was made to receive them; and the solemn ratification of the Covenant between Jahweh the God of Israel and His People[2] must be inferred from the after events of their history to have taken place at the same time.

From Horeb to the disgrace of Baal-peor above the banks of Jordan[3] there is another great hiatus in the records. The memory of a prolonged halt at Kadesh-barnea must not be accepted without hesitation, since the familiarity of Israel with this place may be the outcome of its later occupation of the Arabah.[4] Nor can it be shown what events, if any, took place here. The sending of the spies was, according to one account, from the *"wilderness of Paran"*:[5] the earthquake which swallowed up Dathan and Abiram may have occurred anywhere in the Wanderings: even the death of Miriam which is explicitly connected with Kadesh can offer no evidence of its truth, for it is found in a late and wholly unreliable document.[6] It might be thought that the dispatch of

---

[1] Exod. xix. 16–19.　　　　　　　　　[2] Exod. xxiv. 1–11.
[3] Num. xxv. 1–5; Deut. iv. 3; Hos. ix. 10.
[4] See Appendix I.
[5] Num. xii. 16; xiii. 3, 26.　　　　　　[6] Num. xx. 1 (P).

ambassadors to the king of Edom which is stated as having been from "*Kadesh, a city in the uttermost part of thy border*"[1] is in another category; but this is far from certain. The narrative which follows relates that the Edomites refused to allow Israel to pass through their territory or even to purchase the water which they required: yet this is expressly denied by the Deuteronomist, with whom the memory of Edom is a pleasant and brotherly one.[2] Both stories, in fact, suggest a *political (ethnic)* aetiology which varies its tone with the relations of Israel to its ancient 'kinsman'. No direct evidence, therefore, can be adduced for the sojourn at Kadesh-barnea,[3] and we are forced to fall back on indirect hints and indications. The tradition of the Spies may be no more than an attempt to explain and validate the dominance of the Edomite clan of Caleb in the heart of Judah;[4] yet it is not impossible that such a reconnaisance was made from the Arabah, and the story of Israel's first repulse "*even unto Hormah*" (Kornub?) seems to confirm it.[5] Moreover, the friendly relations which existed between the Israelites and the Kenites whose stronghold seems to have been at Sela (Petra)[6] is best explained by some association of the two peoples in more ancient times. The 'Kadesh-barnea' tradition is, in short, a conjectural probability; and the very fact that this should be so, is a sign that no memorable incident took place there.

The drying-up of the bed of Jordan and the spon-

---

[1] Num. xx. 14 f.   [2] Deut. ii. 6 f., 26–9; xxiii. 7–8.

[3] For the water-miracle at Meribah, see above, p. 65 f.

[4] Num. xiv. 30–8; Deut. i. 36; cf. Joshua xiv. 6–15; xv. 14–19.

[5] Num. xiv. 45. The 'devotion' of Hormah (Devoted) by Israel (Num. xxi. 1–3) is, of course, the merest aetiology: it is extraordinary that some scholars have persisted in arguing from it a successful invasion of the Negeb at this period in the Wanderings.   [6] See Appendix I.

taneous collapse of the walls of Jericho were the final miracles which attested the Call of Israel; and since the material evidence for them which has recently been discovered will be discussed in the following chapter, no more need be said about them here. With them the great Tradition may be said to close; for with this last episode it crowned the glories of the Exodus. It was thus that the Chosen People, freed by the strokes of a superhuman Arm, guided miraculously, covenanted in flame and thunder, watered from the rock and fed from the air,[1] entered at last upon its Heritage.

What impression does this astonishing series of events leave upon us? Our first reaction will normally be one of incredulity. It is not merely that such a succession of stupendous happenings is in itself its own worst enemy for, if these are 'good things', there seems to be certainly a great deal too much of them. It is much more, perhaps, that the garb in which they are now clothed is very often little better than sheer fantasy. The lengthy instructions issued by word of mouth to Moses on the Mount; the Tables written by the very Finger of God; the descending and rising Pillar of Cloud designating the camping-ground of Israel and giving the signal for their advance—it is these and similar descriptions which create a very natural distrust of the narrative and bring under the same condemnation whole regions of it which are in fact quite innocent of this offence.

[1] The 'floating' traditions of the Manna and the Quails are authenticated by this very lack of definition. That the 'Manna' was not originally thought of as a kind of bread is to be inferred from Num. xi. 5 where the people hunger for the old 'relishes', "*leeks and onions and garlick*". The usual explanation of these two phenomena is probably correct, see Driver, pp. 153, 148.

Ne tot mençonge ne tot voir, [vrai]
Tot folie, ne tot savoir;
Tant ont li conteor conté
Et li fableor tant fablé,
Pour lor contes embeleter
Que tout ont fait fables sembler.[1]

Yet if, on the other hand, we resist the temptation to find 'fable' everywhere in the story, it is remarkably easy to arrive at what is virtually the same conclusion from a direction diametrically opposite! While there has been, in fact, among critics, a sincere effort to combat the old incredulity by discovering a 'rational' basis for these phenomena, this process of reducing them to scientific terms has too often resulted in reducing them to nothing. To call such explanations 'rational' is to be guilty of a profound error of judgement. A 'rational' explanation must be one which covers all the known and relevant facts; and among these facts, even among the foremost of them, must be placed, as we have seen, the extra-ordinary contrast between the Israels of Egypt and of Canaan. The more we study this contrast, the more evident does it become that no explanation of the inter-vening events can be considered plausible, which reduces them to the insignificance of everyday occurrences. The more, on the other hand, we examine the Tradition, the more clearly does it reveal itself as satisfying all the conditions of the problem. However wrong its religious interpretation of the events may be—and this, too, remains to be tested—there can be no question that *provided the phenomena themselves are capable of a scientific explanation which does not minimize them* they are precisely of the kind

[1] Wace, *Geste des Bretons*.

which we have been almost constrained to expect. For the Faith of Israel is a miracle which even now shows no signs of ending: and it is by the test of 'miracle' that we shall find out where it began.

ADDITIONAL NOTE ON HOREB–SINAI

The name Sinai is so much more familiar than Horeb that it is usually accepted as an original part of the Tradition. (Actually S. occurs 35 times in O.T., and H. 17, of which 9 are Deut.) Against this, however, there are serious objections. If S. belongs, as is thought, to the Jahwist or Judean source, how comes it that it is H. not S. which is mentioned in the installation of the Ark in the Temple (1 Kings viii. 9—2 Chron. v. 10): and how is it that H. was used by a Levite writer in the Persian period (Mal. iv. 4)? The truth appears to be, rather, that the repeated mention of S. was a deliberate effort to popularize a new, not an ancient, name, and that in reality it is a post-cxilic interpolation. The occurrences of the name are as follows:— Neh. ix. 13 (late post-exilic); Ps. lxviii. 8, 17 (post-exilic in its present form echoing gloss in Judges v. 4–5); Judges v. 5 (an interpolated gloss which is 'metrically superfluous', Burney, p. 117); Deut. xxxiii. 2 (in a late, probably post-exilic, introduction to the Blessing; echoes Judges v. 5; note also '*Meribah of Kadesh*', a sure sign of P); 12 times in Num. (all certainly P); 5 times in Lev. (all certainly P): 13 times in Exod., of which 5 are certainly P, viz. xvi. 1; xix. 1, 2; xxiv. 16 (note the expression '*the top of the Mount*' as typical of P); xxxi. 18 (note '*Tables of Testimony*' as typical of P). S. occurs 4 times in Exod. xxxiv. Two passages (xxxiv. 9, 32) refer to Moses' descent with the second Tables, and both in their present form are P ('*Ts. of Test.*, &c.), but LXX omits S. in verse 29, so that this may be an earlier narrative re-edited: the other two (Exod. xxxiv. 2, 4) relate M.'s ascent to receive these Tables. (Note '*the top of the Mount*' in verse 2 as pointing, but not decisively, to P.) The remaining 4 references concern the Theophany (xix) and here the variations of LXX show clearly how useless the ordinary critical tests can be. (1) The Divine Names are constantly interchanged, viz. in verses 7, 8, 18, 21, 23, 24, where M.T. reads Jahweh, LXX reads Elohim (θεός); all usually assigned to J. (2) The name S. itself is inserted by LXX in verses 16 and 17; both usually assigned to E. Of the 4 references 2 (xix. 20, 23) occur in 'one of the most remarkable instances of redactional work to be met with in the O.T.' (McNeile, p. 113): note also '*the top of the Mount*' (verse 20) and the otherwise unheard-of command that *Aaron* shall ascend the Mount with M. (verse 24): the former indefinitely, the latter decisively, P. There are thus out of 35 references only 3 which are not unambiguously post-exilic. When we consider this evidence, remembering how easily the name could be inserted, and when we note the insistence on it shown in xix by LXX, the conclusion seems inevitable that it is a new name introduced for a deliberate purpose by post-exilic writers.

A probable explanation of their interest in Sinai is that, at some period since the earlier tradition was written down, the mysterious Mount of God had been identified with a particular mountain bearing the name of *Sinai*. That this did actually happen may be inferred from P's itinerary (summarized in Num. xxxiii. 1–49), which would appear to be wholly pointless, unless it was composed as a real guide to the Wanderings. The partially successful identification of its stages by modern explorers is, indeed, most readily explained by the fact that they have followed precisely those indications which they were meant to follow, and have as a result found the Mount of God where they were meant to find it, i.e. in the Sinai Peninsula. It is true that we have no documentary evidence for this identification before the Christian Era, but that does not mean that it was not familiar to Jewry long before: indeed it is not impossible that it suggested itself for the first time, when the navies of Solomon became acquainted with the Red Sea littoral; for it was during that 'Augustan' epoch of Israelite history that the traditions of the Past were arousing special interest (see Appendix I).

If Elim is to be identified with the modern port of Tor which was once called 'Palms' (see below, p. 126, n. 1), the peninsula may have become even better known to Israel through some Solomonic expedition to the turquoise and copper mines of the interior; and reports would quickly follow of the awe-inspiring grandeur of Jebel Serbal or Jebel Musa. Finally, if this great group of mountains was at that time called 'Sinai', the similarity of the name to the Bush (*Seneh*) at which Moses received his call would sooner or later initiate a tradition; and this, though it could hardly be admitted into the documents at so early a date, would have become sufficiently venerable by the days of the post-exilic writers to be accepted by them as a dogmatic truth. The identification of Kadesh-barnea with Sela-Petra seems to have followed the same course, from its beginnings in the Solomonic occupation of the Arabah to its definite acceptance by Ezekiel and all post-exilic and rabbinical writers. (See Appendix I, and Trumbull, *Kadesh-barnea*, 1884, pp. 167 ff.) It only remains to add that the original Tradition knows nothing of this identification of the Mount of God with Sinai, for it places it, with the name of Horeb, in the land of Midian, i.e. to the east of the Arabah and the Gulf of Akaba.

ADDITIONAL NOTE ON THE 'DIVINE PRESENCE'

The intimate connexion between the historical vicissitudes of the Ark and the successive 'doctrines of the Divine Presence' which have so confused the present narrative of Exodus and Numbers,

will perhaps be made clearer in the following diagram, in which
the words in **heavy type** represent the 'focus' of the Presence:

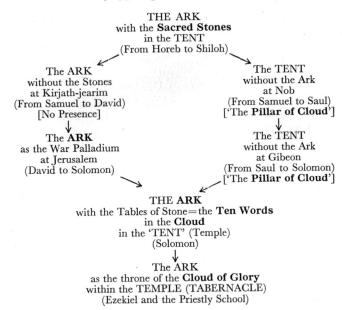

THE ARK
with the **Sacred Stones**
in the TENT
(From Horeb to Shiloh)

The ARK
without the Stones
at Kirjath-jearim
(From Samuel to David)
[No Presence]

The TENT
without the Ark
at Nob
(From Samuel to Saul)
['The **Pillar of Cloud**']

The **ARK**
as the War Palladium
at Jerusalem
(David to Solomon)

The TENT
without the Ark
at Gibeon
(From Saul to Solomon)
['The **Pillar of Cloud**']

THE **ARK**
with the Tables of Stone = the **Ten Words**
in the **Cloud**
in the 'TENT' (Temple)
(Solomon)

The ARK
as the throne of the **Cloud of Glory**
within the TEMPLE (TABERNACLE)
(Ezekiel and the Priestly School)

It would appear probable from 1 Kings viii. 9 that new Tables,
inscribed with the Ten Words, were placed in the Ark before its
enthronement in the Temple. All four conceptions of the Divine
Presence would thus for a time have existed side by side. It will
be noted, however, that as the moral significance of the Ten
Words came increasingly to be emphasized by the prophets, their
'numinous' significance would imperceptibly evaporate, and it
would become a matter of little concern by whose hand they were
originally inscribed upon the Tables of Stone. These Tables
themselves would then in turn recede more and more into the
background, till in the end the more mysterious Cloud could
entirely usurp their place as the 'focus' of the Divine Glory, and
the Ark which contained them be thought of merely as the throne
above which It abode.

PART III

THE MIRACLE OF THE CALL

Chapter I

THE MIRACLES OF JORDAN AND HOREB

IN the investigation of a group of unexplained phenomena there is only one scientific method of attack, to
proceed from the known to the unknown. It is this principle which will determine the starting-point of our
present inquiry, for while the series of miracles which
is to be examined extends chronologically from the banks
of the Nile through the Wilderness to the banks of the
Jordan, there is only one point at which it makes clear
contact with modern knowledge and that point happens
to fall at the end. In the following pages, therefore, we
shall study these events in their reverse order, and we
shall begin with the record of the extraordinary phenomena which preceded and accompanied the Fall of
Jericho.

1. THE DRYING-UP OF THE JORDAN.

The documentary tradition records that on the
approach of the Sacred Ark to the brink of the river:

> "*The waters which came down from above stood, and rose
> up in one heap, a great way off, at Adam, the city that is
> beside Zarethan: and those that went down toward the sea of
> the Arabah, even the Salt Sea, were wholly cut off: and the
> people passed over right against Jericho. And the priests that
> bare the ark of the covenant of Jahweh stood firm on dry
> ground in the midst of Jordan, and all Israel passed over on
> dry ground. . . ."* [1]

[1] Joshua iii. 16–17.

The physical explanation of this miracle has now been clearly demonstrated. At the site of Damieh (the ancient Adameh), sixteen miles up the river from Jericho, the bed of the Jordan is liable to be entirely blocked by great landslides from the overhanging banks. Professor Garstang records instances of this in 1267 and 1906, but the most recent and notable occasion was in 1927, when as a result of the several earthquakes of that year, 'a section of the cliff, which here rises to a height of 150 feet, fell bodily across the river and completely dammed it, so that no water flowed down the river bed for twenty-one and a half hours. . . . During this time, it is asserted by several living witnesses that they crossed and recrossed the bed of the river freely on foot.'[1]

That the walls of Jericho, which were found to have collapsed forward down the slope of the city mound, were shaken from their badly-laid foundations by the same physical cause is regarded by Garstang as probable though incapable of proof.[2] Clear evidence of seismic activity was visible within the town itself, and there can be no doubt that Jericho suffered several times in its history from its situation in the geologically unstable rift of the Jordan Valley. The full significance of these facts will be appreciated later: at the moment it will be enough to stress the remarkable agreement between the Tradition (even in its present recorded form) and the scientific explanation which recent discoveries have provided. It is not merely that the traditional topography of the miracle is confirmed by the evidence of later centuries. It is much more that *the scale of this explanation is commensurate with the impression which the phenomenon itself created.* Here on the one side we find the memory of what was believed to be

[1] Garstang, *Joshua, Judges*, p. 136 f.   [2] Ib., p. 404.

a great Divine Intervention; of an event, in other words, so abnormal and unearthly in its magnitude that only a miraculous interpretation was thought adequate to account for it: while on the other we can offer, from our knowledge of the same locality, the evidence of those mighty subterranean convulsions in the throes of which not only Man, but Earth herself, is powerless. This point, as we have seen above, is of exceptional importance. Many modern critical efforts to account rationally for the miracles of the Exodus may be aptly compared to an attempt to open a gigantic cathedral lock with a Yale key: there is, in short, a disproportion between the problem and its solution so palpably enormous that it merely provokes in us a sense of helpless exasperation. Here, however, at the outset the key is quite obviously of the same scale as the lock, and when, on proceeding to test their agree-ment in detail, we find that at point after point they fit together with extraordinary precision, we have no need to hesitate in claiming success for our experiment and may be satisfied that in our progress towards the truth this door at least is open.

But this is not all. To have established the solution of the last event in our series has a twofold importance in view of the more difficult task which lies ahead. As a proof of the substantial accuracy of the Tradition, it encourages the hope that the rest of the series will yield to a similar treatment, while in drawing our attention to the appositeness of a particular class of phenomena it defines clearly the probable range of our inquiry. The ground gained by this initial step is, in fact, far more than we might reasonably have anticipated. We advance from it with a new confidence and with eyes that have attained a truer focus. For if the scale of the miracles of the Exodus is admittedly colossal, we shall be prepared to meet them with phenomena no less stupendous. We have already made trial of one of these, the Earthquake; we have now to encounter a second, the Volcano.

2. THE PILLAR OF CLOUD AND FIRE.

"And Jahweh went before them by day in a pillar of cloud, to lead them the way; and by night in a pillar of fire, to give them light; that they might go by day and by night; the pillar of cloud by day, and the pillar of fire by night, departed not from before the people."[1]

Of all the miraculous phenomena which accompanied the Exodus this mysterious Pillar seems the first to demand an explanation. No other incident in the Wanderings of Israel has left so deep an impression upon its Tradition as this vast Signal of Deliverance which guided the People unrestingly to the Mount of God. So strong indeed was the awe which the memory of it inspired that it could be conceived by later thought as the vehicle of the Divine Presence, whether descending in the sight of all men to the door of the Tabernacle or hovering in mysterious darkness over the Mercy Seat in the Most Holy Place.[2]

What explanation, then, are we to offer of this apparently supernatural phenomenon? It must be clear, at least, on what level our answer lies; since the Pillar must have been deemed miraculous in the first place precisely for the reason that no ordinary manifestations of Nature, *as they were then known*, were competent to explain it.[3] To-day our knowledge is in better case, and

---

[1] Exod. xiii. 21.   [2] See above, pp. 118 and 134.

[3] The usual explanation of the phenomenon is the 'variously attested custom of a brazier filled with burning wood being borne along at the head

we are able to supply a perfectly natural interpretation of what to Israel appeared a divine prodigy. There is, in fact, one obvious explanation of this miracle, an explanation so rational and so complete that it ought long ago to have won universal acceptance: that it was nothing else than one of those enormous columns of dust and steam and ashes which are projected, sometimes to almost incredible heights, from the open mouth of a violently active volcano.[1]

'Of all volcanic phenomena, the most constant is the emission of vapour. It is one of the earliest features of an eruption . . . attaining often to a prodigious volume. . . . During a violent eruption the vapour may be suddenly shot upwards *as a vertical column of enormous height*, penetrating the passing clouds. . . . In a great eruption the height of the mountain itself may appear dwarfed by comparison with that of the column of vapour. During the eruption of Vesuvius in April 1906, the steam and dust rose to a height of between 6 and 8 miles. At Krakatoa, in 1883, the column of vapour and ashes reached an altitude of nearly 20 miles.'[2]

It is true that the Israelite records in their present form mention the appearance of the Pillar at the moment of the people's departure from the Land of Goshen; and since the volcanic fields of Midian are at least 300 miles distant

of a caravan of pilgrims, or an army, or of a chief having a fire blazing before his tent.' Driver, *Exodus*, 1918, p. 113; cf. McNeile, p. 82. For a far more 'adequate' explanation, which fails, nevertheless, to satisfy all the conditions of the problem, see C. S. Jarvis, *Yesterday and To-day in Sinai*, 1931, p. 179.

[1] The volcanic hypothesis is no new one. It was suggested as long ago as 1873 by Prof. Charles Beke, although he ultimately withdrew from this position. It was accepted *inter alios* by Gunkel, Eduard Meyer, and Gressmann and more recently by Robinson.

[2] *Enc. Brit.*, 11th ed., Vol. XXVIII, p. 179, s.v. 'Volcano'. The italics are the present writer's.

from Suez,[1] it might seem as if this explanation were rendered untenable from the outset. But this is precisely one of those cases where a too great readiness to trust the details of the narrative may lead the student astray. The *basis* of the Tradition, its substantial feature, is the appearance of the Pillar to the Israelites whilst on the march from Egypt. Actually they may have caught sight of it for the first time much later in their journey, but the impression it created must almost inevitably have tended to enhance and extend its dramatic range, not only backwards to the frontier of Egypt, but forwards (as we actually find it in the later sources) to the very borders of the Promised Land. There is, moreover, one curious piece of evidence which seems to make it not altogether incredible that a phenomenon of this type could be visible at an enormous distance. In A.D. 1256 there was a violent eruption in the volcanic fields east of Medina, and we learn from the Arab writer al-Mukrizi that the 'flames' of this eruption (i.e. the reflection of the molten lava in the clouds above the crater) could be seen as far as the environs of Bozrah, 600 miles distant, in the Hauran.[2] If this testimony cannot be accepted as wholly reliable, it is at least of peculiar interest for our inquiry, for the volcanic fields east of the Gulf of Akaba are not much more than half that number of miles from the western borders of Egypt.

3. THE MOUNT OF GOD (*First Phase*).

The identification of the Pillar of Cloud and Fire with the 'stone-pine' column of an erupting volcano makes

---

[1] They are to-day called the Harras and extend along the eastern side of the Gulf of Akaba from a little south of Tebuk to Medina. The whole district now falls within the Northern Hejaz. See below, Appendix II, and map facing page 214.   [2] Musil, *The Northern Hejaz*, 1926, p. 316.

instantly clear much that has hitherto remained a mystery. Since it was this column of vapour and ashes which led Israel unerringly to the Mount of God, it follows in all probability that it was from the summit of that Mount that the Pillar issued; in other words, that Horeb itself was a volcano. Further support for this hypothesis is immediately forthcoming. It is generally held that this title, the 'Mount of God', belonged to Horeb before Moses first happened upon it in his pastoral wanderings;[1] that Horeb, in fact, had been venerated as a holy mountain long before its connexion with the story of Israel. It has been inferred from this that the mountain was sacred to one of the gods of Midian, and upon this slender assumption as a base, a theory of the Midianite origin of Jahwism has been precariously erected. Such a theory —quite apart from the collapse of its other main support, the story of Jethro's visit and sacrifice[2]—will now be seen to have become not merely unnecessary but irrelevant. This vaguely mysterious title, the 'Mount of God', need have no connexion with the normal pantheon of Midianite divinities; rather it will reflect the awe inspired by the spectacle of this strange mountain, aloof and terrible, where nameless powers slumbered, or awoke only to destroy.

That this was in fact the origin of the name may be deduced from the description of Moses' first visit to Horeb.[3] He had wandered, as an ignorant foreigner, upon ground which had always been treated as *taboo*. Suddenly some strange fiery phenomenon caught his eye, and as he advanced towards it, the rumble of an

---

[1] Driver, *Exodus*, p. 18; McNeile, p. 15.
[2] See above, p. 72 f.
[3] Exod. iii. 1–5.

unearthly voice halted him in his tracks.[1] Of other physical manifestations we hear nothing, but the picture as it stands is that of a volcano long venerated (and avoided) because of its mysterious fires and now, though not yet active, in that semi-quiescent stage which precedes eruption. That such a mountain might be named 'the Mount of God' by the people in whose borders it stood, is not merely a conjecture but a fact which can be verified. Two thousand miles away to the south on the western edge of the great Rift Valley of East Africa, which we shall find later playing an unexpected role in our inquiry, there stands a mountain which is deeply venerated to this day by the tribes of the Masai who dwell around it. Like Horeb in the age of Moses, it is holy

---

[1] The most natural explanation of the 'Burning Bush' is that it was some electrical phenomenon due to volcanic activity—'The abundant generation of atmospheric electricity is a familiar phenomenon in all volcanic eruptions on a large scale' (*The Eruption of Krakatoa. Report of the Committee of the Royal Society*, 1888, p. 21). *Corposants* (St. Elmo's Fires) were observed on ships 40 miles distant from the eruption of Krakatoa. One captain records the occurrence of 'a peculiar pinky flame coming from clouds which seemed to touch the mast-heads and yard-arms', and another says that the mud-rain, which covered the masts, rigging, and decks, was phosphorescent, and that the native crew regarded the light as the work of evil spirits (ib., p. 20 f.). On the other hand, the occurrence of such a light at the Mount of God would seem to require *an active eruption*, and not only does the narrative not suggest this, but it is difficult to understand Moses' presence at the Mount if the volcano was already becoming violent. It is, however, possible that the tradition has been slightly distorted. A recently published photograph from the Copsa region of Transylvania shows an enormous column of flame (actually 900 ft. high) leaping up out of the earth in the middle of a grass-covered orchard, while two women are quietly at work a few hundred yards away. The fire, which issued from one large vent, is said to be due to 'the ignition of inflammable gases emanating from the crater of an extinct volcano' (*The Sphere*, Aug. 12th, 1933, p. 243). Such a phenomenon, encountered in the middle of a wilderness shunned by man, might well arouse the awe, and stir the heart, of Moses.

ground, *taboo*; like Horeb, when Israel encamped beneath it, no flocks or herds are permitted to graze about its foot. This African mountain is a volcano which was in active eruption as recently as 1917; and its name is Oldonyo Ngai (or Lengai), 'the Mount of God'.[1]

4. THE MOUNT OF GOD (*Last Phase*).

That the Sacred Mountain burst into full eruption after the return of Moses to Egypt has already been attested by the Pillar of Cloud and Fire. (This phenomenon, it will have been noted, is one of the 'earliest features' of an eruption.)[2] Whether the paroxysms were continuous, or, as is so often the case, intermittent, we have no means of telling, for it is impossible to judge the length of time which was consumed by the forced marches of Israel from the Red Sea to Horeb. One thing, however, is quite clear from the existing evidence of the Tradition, that at some period during the People's sojourn at the Mount, a terrific and awe-inspiring outburst took place:

> "*There were thunders and lightnings, and a thick cloud upon the mount, and the voice of a trumpet exceeding loud; and all the people that were in the camp trembled. And Moses brought forth the people out of the camp to meet God; and they stood at the nether part of the mount. And [the] mount . . . was altogether on smoke, because Jahweh descended upon it in fire; and the smoke thereof ascended as the smoke of a furnace,*

[1] T. A. Barnes, *Across the Great Craterland to the Congo*, 1923, pp. 57–8. The same *taboo* is reported by Musil (*N.H.*, p. 215) as having been attached by the Bedouin to the holy volcano of el-Bedr (Tadra) which stands on the edge of the lava-fields of Midian and may well be the Mount of God itself. See below, pp. 152–4 and Appendix II.

[2] Technically, the stage of moderate or Strombolian activity, while the full eruption is known as the paroxysmal (Vesuvian) phase.

L

and the whole mount quaked greatly. And when the voice of the trumpet waxed louder and louder, Moses spake, and God answered him by a voice.[1]

A comparison of the phenomena recorded in this passage with those which have been observed in the course of great volcanic eruptions will leave little doubt as to the character of the Mount of God.   There were, in the first place:

(*a*) *"Thunders and lightnings, and a thick cloud."* Those who have not studied, or had personal knowledge of, volcanic eruptions will probably be unaware that, in the course of these, terrific electric storms continually flash and thunder in the thick cloud which overhangs the crater. We need only quote one writer on the subject of these storms, the absence of which would have been more notable than their presence. 'The electrical phenomena attending an eruption are often of great intensity and splendour.   The dark, ash-laden clouds of vapour are shot through and through by volcanic lightning, sometimes in rapid horizontal flashes, then in oblique forked streaks, or again in tortuous lines compared to fiery serpents.'[2]   That the thunders and lightnings of the Mount of God did not proceed from an ordinary passing thunder-storm is clear from what follows.   There was also:

(*b*) *"The voice of a trumpet exceeding loud."* A trumpet will suggest to a modern reader some kind of musical instrument, but all that the expression was intended to convey was that there proceeded from the *"thick cloud"* a tremendously loud and piercing blast, and it is said that this

[1] Exod. xix. 16–19.   On the question of the critical analysis see Additional Note on Horeb–Sinai, p. 131.
[2] *Enc. Brit.*, loc. cit., p. 179.

noise was repeated and that it "*waxed louder and louder*". Here again a parallel is not far to seek. Observers of the eruption of Stromboli in 1915 describe one of the vents which opened near the centre of activity as blowing off 'at intervals of from 20 to 40 minutes with a loud, startlingly sudden blast like a steam whistle from a gigantic locomotive'.[1] The choice of similes reflects the interval of 3,000 years which separates the two accounts: in essentials they are clearly indistinguishable.

(c) "*The smoke ascended as the smoke of a furnace and the whole mount quaked greatly.*" One daring observer who ascended Mont Pelée the day before its second great eruption of 1902 describes its convulsions as follows: 'There were no accentuated detonations but a continuous roar that was simply appalling. . . . No words can describe it. Were it possible to unite all the furnaces of the globe into a single one, and to simultaneously let loose (*sic!*) their blasts of steam, it does not seem to me that such a sound could be produced. . . . The mountain fairly quivered under its work.'[2]

(d) Lastly, *for the general impression* which such a spectacle inevitably creates, we may quote the words of Dr. F. A. Perrett, who witnessed the great eruption of Vesuvius on April 6th, 1906. The whole mountain, he says, hummed and vibrated like a gigantic boiler under a colossal pressure of steam, and he records the emotions which this tremendous spectacle aroused, in the following words:

'Strongest of all impressions received in the course of these remarkable events, greatest of all surprises, and most gratifying of all features to record was, for the writer, that of an infinite dignity in every manifestation of this stupendous

[1] G. W. Tyrrell, *Volcanoes*, 1931, p. 85.
[2] A. Heilprin, *Mount Pelée and the Tragedy of Martinique*, 1903, p. 227.

releasing of energy. No words can describe the majesty of its unfolding, the utter absence of anything resembling effort, and the all-sufficient power to perform the allotted task and to do it majestically. Each rapid impulse was the crest of something deep and powerful and uniform which bore it, and the unhurried modulation of its rhythmic beats sets this eruption in the rank of things which are mighty, grave, and great.

'There was present also the element of awe, in all its fulness. The phenomena entered, through their intensity, that sphere where the normal conditions of Nature are over-passed, and one stands in the presence of greater and more elemental forces than any he has known hitherto. This tends to induce a state of mind which hardly recognizes as en-tirely natural this transformation of the visible universe, and with difficulty one accepts the dictum of reason, that all will pass and the normal return as before.'[1]

It is not hard, after reading these words of a modern scientist, to estimate the overwhelming psychological effect which such a phenomenon must have produced in the hearts of the Israelites. Now for the first time we can begin, however dimly, to discern the source of that undying belief in a divinely guided destiny which through so many centuries rallied and inspired the 'Chosen People'. Even had the memory of this awful and majestic spectacle been all that they carried away from the "*Mount that burned with fire*", it must have been enough to stamp upon their minds one great imperishable conviction, that they, of all mankind, had heard the very voice of God, and lived.[2] Yet this experience—immense though its effects must have been—was no more than the prelude to the tremendous drama of the Covenant. It

---

[1] Dr. F. A. Perrett (Tyrrell, op. cit., p. 147 f.).   [2] Deut. iv. 33.

was no mere memory which the flames and thunders of Horeb were to impart to Israel, but something even more precious, a visible material token of their Divine Election.

5. THE TABLES OF STONE.

It was, as we have seen, the consistent belief of Israel that when Moses returned from his converse with God in the thick darkness he brought with him two inscribed Tables of Stone. The earliest tradition with regard to these was that they were both hewn and written upon by God Himself, and the most obvious explanation of this legend is that they were in some way associated with the fires of the burning mount and that they bore upon their surface the appearance of an unearthly script. Here again we have no need to go far to find an explanation which will satisfy both these conditions:

'When a volcano after a long period of repose starts into fresh activity, the materials which have accumulated in the crater . . . have to be ejected. . . . Such ejected blocks, by no means uncommon in the early stages of an eruption, are often of large size and naturally vary according to the character of the rocks through which the duct has been opened. They may be irregular masses of igneous rocks, possibly lavas of earlier eruptions, *or they may be stratified, sedimentary and fossiliferous rocks* representing the platform on which the volcano has been built.'[1]

The words italicized (by the present writer) are of peculiar interest. They suggest the possibility of a phenomenon precisely similar to that which the Tradition requires; that, namely, of a 'slate' or 'table' of some fissile rock, bearing on its surface a series or group of

[1] *Enc. Brit.*, loc. cit., p. 180.

apparently significant 'characters'. When to these mysterious and certainly non-human 'signs' we add that strange transformation in texture and appearance which such a block or 'bomb' must necessarily undergo from the effect of the volcanic fires, we have arrived within measurable distance of the solution of our problem. Finally, it is reasonable to suppose that these 'signs', though clearly written by no human hand, nevertheless conveyed a meaning to Moses and must therefore have *simulated* some script known to him; and it is not wholly idle to conjecture that this script was the primitive Semitic alphabet and that the 'characters' upon the Tables spelled out the Sacred Name.[1] Certainly on this assumption we obtain a simple and perfectly natural explanation of the events which followed. If Moses accepted these Tables—as what man in that age and in the midst of such a scene would not?—for that which they seemed to proclaim themselves so clearly, the sign-manual of Jahweh given out of the heart of the fire, was it not inevitable that he should carry them down, rejoicing, to his people? For Israel these visible signs of the Covenant would be of untold value; not, as the later writers thought, because they contained some written code of laws, but for the very mystery which clothed them and for the simple and solid fact of their existence. From that day onwards the Sacred Ark which held them must have become for every faithful Israelite the focus of his faith and adoration; for there, by the testimony of all who had stood before the Mount, there lay concealed the

---

[1] The earliest known example of this script in Canaan occurs on a pottery fragment of the Middle Bronze Age (*c.* 2000–1600 B.C.) found at Gezer. The Sinaitic inscriptions seem to be contemporary. See Olmstead, *History of Palestine and Syria*, 1931, p. 93.

tangible evidence of Divine favour; the warrant, nay the very Angel, of the Nation's destiny.[1]

We are now in a position to summarize the results so far attained. First, we may regard it as a fact established beyond dispute that the drying up of the Jordan and (if only indirectly) the collapse of the walls of Jericho had, *as their physical cause*, one of those terrible and dreaded earthquakes which work havoc from time to time in the Jordan Valley and its environs. That the whole of this region was at that period undergoing not one but a series of such convulsions is not improbable, for it can be no mere coincidence that the tradition of the Wanderings records the occurrence of a similar catastrophe in or about the neighbourhood of the same Rift to the south of the Dead Sea.[2] The full bearing of this will become evident later, but, before considering it, we must deal with the second of our immediate problems, the Mount of God.

If the arguments which have been advanced in proof of the volcanic hypothesis have carried conviction to the reader, it may yet appear to him unreasonable to accept it until it has been corroborated by the evidence of geography. That evidence must of necessity fall short of absolute certainty. It is impossible, for example, to prove that at a particular period of history a particular volcano in Midian was in course of eruption. But it must at least be demonstrated that such a volcano actually existed in these parts and that it was not one of those which have been extinct since geological times.

Here a glance at the map will reveal some interesting results. While the Sinai peninsula, which seems in later

[1] *P.E.F.Q.S.*, 1930, p. 148.   [2] Num. xvi (Dathan and Abiram).

centuries to have usurped the glory of the true Mount
of God, is wholly destitute of any volcanic remains, it is
far otherwise with those regions which were once the
Land of Midian.[1] It is true that the exact boundaries of
that nation are uncertain, but all the available evidence
goes to show that the Midianites controlled the great
trade-routes from South Arabia to Damascus and that
their territory was coextensive with at least a part of the
lofty plateau of the Northern Hejaz.[2] The southernmost of their settlements hitherto known was the oasis
of Dedan, the modern el-Ala (26·37° N.: 38·26° E.) and
to the north-west and west of this extend the great lava-
fields called the Harras, from the midst of which rise
innumerable volcanic craters. Of one of these, Dr. Alois
Musil, who passed close to it, heard so strange a tale from
his guides, that if his informants had not been wild
Bedouin, it would have been natural to dismiss it
instantly as a sheer fabrication. This volcano—its name
is Hala el-Bedr—rises upon the eastern slope of a grey
'table-mountain' called Tadra or Tedhara (27·15° N. :
37·10° E.). It is regarded as holy by the Beli tribe, in
whose territory it lies. At its foot, so the guides said, there
is a 'sacred spot called el-Manhal and upon it are twelve
stones known as el-Madbah, where the Beli still offer up
sacrifices when they are encamped close by.[3] Tadra and
the entire surrounding district is associated with various
legends. The volcano of el-Bedr is said once to have
vomited fire and stones, destroying many Bedouins and
their camels and sheep. Since then the Bedouins have

[1] See Map, p. 186. For a fuller discussion of the subject see below,
Appendix II.

[2] See below, Appendix II. For a very full examination of the Midianites and their land see Musil, *N.H.*, Appendix IX.

[3] Cf. Exod. xxiv. 4–5.

been afraid to ascend this volcano and they drive away their animals, not allowing them to graze upon the slopes or upon the grey ridge of Tadra.'[1] Musil was told of the existence of 'various signs and inscriptions' on the sacrificial boulders of el-Manhal, but was unable to visit the spot owing to the exhaustion of his party. The Arabs also reported that on the western slope of the mountain there used to flow a spring which has now been clogged by the collapse of a rock.[2] Finally, in a neighbouring volcano there were said to be caves called 'The Caves of the Servants of Moses', and the guide explained this name by the fact that 'the servants of Moses sojourned there when their master was abiding with Allah'.[3]

It is unfortunate in the extreme that information of such extraordinary interest should still lack scientific verification, for if only a part of this report be true, the site of Horeb is surely settled for all time. It may, indeed, be objected to this identification, after a first scrutiny of the map, that it places the Mount of God much too far to the south, and that it is 'inconceivable' that Israel should ever have travelled such a distance from the Land of Goshen. But a moment's thought will show that this argument is really irrational. We required a volcano within the territory of Midian and we have found it: we cannot, then, in fairness complain if its location does not agree with certain of our preconceived ideas. Rather must we argue that if *this* volcano is indeed the ancient Horeb, we shall merely be constrained to readjust our conception of the distances covered by Israel. Meanwhile the matter must remain in the tantalizing realm of

---

[1] Musil, *N.H.*, p. 215. For the *taboo* cf. Exod. xix. 12–13, and see above on Oldonyo Ngai, p. 144.

[2] Cf. Exod. xvii. 5–6.   [3] Musil, *N.H.*, p. 214.

speculation and we must content ourselves with a more modest conclusion. If we cannot as yet say definitely that we have discovered Horeb, we can at least claim to be able to show where it is to be found. *Somewhere* within the confines of those gaunt volcanic plateaux the Mount of God slumbers in solitude, its work accomplished, and its ancient peace restored.

Chapter II

THE MIRACLES OF THE PLAGUES AND RED SEA

IF the conclusions so far attained have met with a reasonable measure of acceptance, two inferences can be drawn which will prove of the greatest value. First, it will be admitted that the 'basis' of the Tradition has been found to be remarkably reliable. The wholly 'undesigned coincidences' which have been noted in the previous chapter would indeed be inexplicable if there had not lain behind them a memory which no later triumphs or misfortunes could efface. We shall be entitled, then, to assume that the record of those earlier events which preceded and accompanied the Exodus may, *in their substance* (when divested of later embellishments and distortions), be trusted without misgivings. Secondly, it will be recognized that the phenomena which created this memory gave it its sharpness and vitality precisely because of their own peculiar and distinctive character. It will be natural, therefore, in examining the story of the Exodus to take as a starting-point the possibility of a similar explanation.

Our first clue, to put it briefly, is concerned with the singular geological structure of the Rift Valley of Jordan, which, continuing southwards through the Arabah into the Red Sea, provides a direct physical connexion between the volcanic paroxysms of Horeb and the seismic shocks which threw open the Promised Land to Israel. The bearing of this fact is of such importance for our problem that it will be necessary to dwell upon it at some length. We shall find that it affords us what may be the only adequate solution of an otherwise incredible 'coincidence'; that it explains, in other words, how the waters of the Nile and the Red Sea could be linked in one series of portents with those of Jordan, and the darkness "*that could be felt*" in all the land of Egypt with the thunders and thick darkness of the Midianite Mount of God.

That there should be any distinct physical connexion between regions so far removed as the highlands of the Northern Hejaz and the sources of the Nile might at first sight appear an idle and even futile proposition. It remains, nevertheless, an observed fact that such a connexion may exist between seismic and volcanic disturbances taking place at great distances from one another and over large areas of the earth's surface.[1] A comparison between the European mediterranean basin and the somewhat similar American mediterranean basin constituted by the Gulf of Mexico and the Caribbean Sea shows that in both these regions we are to recognize areas of marked and long-existing weakness of the earth's crust, in which breakages have been progressively taking place and are still continuing. Around these 'regions of weakness' great ridges have been thrown up, and it is in association with the breakage of these that seismic and volcanic disturbances are found to occur. The boundaries of these regions may be widely separated. Those of the 'region of weakness' which is included within, or touched by, the Caribbean Gulf basin

'may be roughly drawn from the western coast of Mexico to the Lesser Antilles . . . and from the northern parts of

---

[1] For what follows the writer is indebted very largely to Prof. Heilprin's account of such phenomena in his work, already cited, upon the tragic eruption of Mont Pelée.

South America to Porto Rico and the lower parts of the Mississipi Valley. As in 1812, the great May 1902 eruption of the Soufrière [of St. Vincent] was preceded by violent seismic disturbances in the northern part of South America, particularly accentuated in Columbia and Venezuela, and, in close chronologic harmony, by the great earthquake which, on April 18, destroyed the city of Quezaltenango in Guatemala, seemingly the most destructive earthquake in the western hemisphere since the one which in 1812 wrecked Caracas.

'There is perhaps nothing that so clearly establishes the unity of the Gulf Caribbean region as a region of far-reaching instability as the broad range of its seismic and volcanic phenomena and the correspondent relations which they teach. No succession of events could present this fact more lucidly than the events of the early part of this year, 1902, when disturbances of one kind or another were developed over a linear area of nearly or quite two thousand five hundred miles, extending from Colima in Mexico on the west, to Martinique in the east. The areal distribution of these occurrences is, indeed, so vast that one is almost prompted to deny the existence of any true relation binding them together; but the evidence obtained from similar concurrent events in former periods of time leaves no doubt that the association, which naturally fastens itself upon the mind, does in fact exist.'[1]

The relevance of these considerations to our present problem can be readily appreciated when we remember that the volcanoes of the Hejazi Harras themselves mark the line of such a 'region of weakness'. The great rift of the Jordan Valley, Dead Sea, Arabah, and Gulf of Akaba is, in fact, the trough of an enormous geological 'fault' bordered at intervals along its entire length by masses of lava from fissure eruptions or by the craters of dormant or extinct volcanoes. At the outset, therefore, there is

[1] Heilprin, op cit., p. 266.

ample reason for suggesting a single common disturbance for the eruption of Horeb and the earthquakes which destroyed Dathan and Abiram, dried up the bed of Jordan, and shook from their foundations the walls of Jericho.

But this is not all; for the Rift which we have so far been considering is found on closer inspection to be no more than the smallest fraction of a far vaster 'fault' which penetrates into the heart of Africa. Its course can be traced along the line of the Red Sea where it is marked by numerous volcanic islands, at least one of which, that of Jebel Teir (or Tair), has only recently become extinct.[1] From this point it turns southwards through the Afar plains of Abyssinia, the Hawash Valley, and the line of lakes which extends from Zwai to Stephanie; thence to Lake Rudolph, and thence again, through the 'Land of the Giant Craters', to Lake Nyasa. Here it meets a similar 'faulted' rift, the great Central African or Albertine trough, which runs up through Lakes Tanganyika Kivu, Edward, and Albert to the volcanic Birunga (or Kirunga) mountains and the sources of the Nile.[2]

'From the Lebanons, therefore, almost to the Cape there runs a valley unique . . . on account of the persistence with which it maintains its trough-like form, throughout the whole course of its 4000 miles. . . . All along the line the natives have traditions of great changes in the structure of the country. The Arabs tell us that the Red Sea is simply water that did not dry up after Noah's deluge. The Somali say that when their ancestors crossed from Arabia to Africa

[1] *Red Sea and Gulf of Aden Pilot*, p. 98. Other volcanic islands noticed in the *Pilot* are Kotenbul, Saba, Disei, Howakil, Kurdumiyat, Zukur, Saddle, Jebel Abayil, and Hanish islands.

[2] J. W. Gregory, *The Rift Valleys and Geology of East Africa*, 1921, pp. 19–23. See Map 1.

there was a land connection between the two, across the straits of Bab el Mandeb. The natives of Ujiji, at the southern end of the line, have a folklore that goes back to the time when Lake Tanganyika was formed by the flooding of a fertile plain, rich in cattle and plantations. And at the northern end of the valley we have the accounts of the destruction of the towns of Sodom and Gomorrah.... There is geological evidence to show that great earth-movements have happened along this Rift Valley . . . at a recent date, which makes it distinctly probable that these traditions are recollections of the geographical changes."[1]

Here then, it would seem, we have yet another 'region of far-reaching instability' comparable in extent with the European and American mediterranean basins. Along almost its entire course this 'fault' is bordered by, and associated with, areas of volcanic activity and seismic disturbance, and although there appears to be no historical evidence of simultaneous outbreaks at far-removed points along it, we have seen that there is no scientific reason for denying the *possibility* of such con-currences in the past. But can we not at this point, without undue rashness, go further? Can it, after all, be a mere coincidence that the area covered by this vast belt of weakness includes, or indirectly affects, precisely those regions where a series of wholly abnormal phenomena is recorded in Israelite tradition as occurring within a comparatively brief space of time? Our answer to this question will depend very largely upon the degree in which it is possible to identify these miracles with the known evidence of seismic or volcanic activity.

What was it, in scientific language, which caused the Plagues? What really happened between the shores of the Red Sea?

[1] J. W. Gregory, *The Great Rift Valley*, 1896, p. 5.

1. The Plagues

From the brief description of the Plagues given in a previous chapter[1] it will be clear that the majority of them are capable of a perfectly natural explanation. The pestilence which raged first among the cattle and finally among the Egyptians themselves is, in fact, accounted for in the record as it stands by the initial disaster which befell the life-giving waters of the Nile. Apart from these, moreover, the destruction wrought upon the crops by the hail and the locusts shows nothing of the abnormal except perhaps in its unusual intensity, and (in respect of the former) the suggestion of some very marked atmospheric disturbance. It is only when we come to consider the Nile-plague itself and the mysterious pall of darkness which followed it that we find ourselves once more in the realm of the truly extraordinary and stupendous, and are forced to seek for a less 'natural' explanation.

(i) Of the first of these 'plagues' the account given is curiously precise and vivid:

> "*All the waters that were in the river were turned to blood. And the fish that was in the river died; . . . and the Egyptians could not drink water from the river.*"[2]

To what miracle are we to ascribe this transformation of the Nile? It is commonly suggested that the phenomenon must be related to the reddening of the river during the summer inundations, the colouring being due to the red marl brought down from the mountains of Abyssinia. The objection to this view is twofold. Not merely is this change of colour a normal and familiar event[3] but it never has the effect of making the water

---

[1] See above, p. 123 f.   [2] Exod. vii. 20–1.
[3] Driver, *Exodus*, p. 62.

unwholesome or undrinkable. Nothing, in fact, could afford a more valuable guarantee of the general reliability of the old tradition. Egypt was for many centuries a familiar country to the Israelites. The story of Joseph, for example, is full of little touches which could only spring from a first-hand acquaintance with its habits and scenery. It is therefore in no small degree surprising to find that the first of the 'Plagues' bears so strong and yet so distorted a resemblance to one of the annual features of Delta life. An inventive imagination would have avoided so obvious a contradiction, and there is therefore a strong presumption in favour of the authenticity of this strange and 'unnatural' visitation. But what can have caused it? What extraordinary event can have been taking place those two thousand miles away around the sources of the Nile? It must have been something which not only had power to pour a vast flow of mud into that mighty stream, but to inject it at the same time with huge quantities of some fetid chemical poison. "*The fish that was in the river died . . . and the river stank.*" The moment we are prepared to take that statement seriously, both the size and the nature of this catastrophe become of vital importance. If such a thing could happen, the hidden cause of it must have been of some wholly abnormal kind, and the forces expended in producing it of almost inconceivable magnitude. It takes rank at once in the class of those earthly happenings which are 'mighty, grave, and great'.

Here once more we may have recourse to the tragic story of Mont Pelée.[1] On May 5th, 1902, a day before the calamitous eruption which destroyed St. Pierre with its 30,000 souls, a terrible torrent of boiling mud was

[1] Heilprin, op. cit., pp. 66, 78–9.

M

suddenly evacuated from one of the lakes upon the mountain and swept down to the shore, overwhelming everything in its course. At about the same time the torrential rains produced by the vast output of steam from the discharging crater turned all the streams on this side of the island into muddy cataracts of black and poisonous water. Great quantities of dead fish were observed later floating at the mouths of these rivers and the smell of sulphur hung overpoweringly over all.

Is it not just such a catastrophe as this which must have occurred in those remote volcanic highlands where the Nile takes its rise? The appalling deluges of mud which follow all great volcanic eruptions are only too well known to those who have had to endure them. 'The Italians, indeed, dread the floods which follow an eruption more than the fiery streams of lava which accompany it—for they have found the mud-streams (*lave di fango*), formed by rain-water sweeping along the loose volcanic materials, to be more widely destructive in their effects than the currents of molten rock (*lave di fuoco*).'[1] It is a Nile fouled by the inrush of such a torrent which is revealed to us as the first instrument of Israel's deliverance.[2]

(ii) The Plague of Darkness is perhaps the most surprising of all the miracles of the Exodus, for though

---

[1] J. W. Judd, *Volcanoes*, 1903, p. 30.

[2] The Kirunga volcanoes were in eruption at the end of the last, and the beginning of the present, century (Gregory, op. cit., 1921, p. 270). It is, however, possible that the cause of the catastrophe was an eruption in the 'apparently recent volcanic area' discovered by Dr. Chalmers Mitchell in the neighbourhood of Bayuda (between Berber and Korti) in the great bend of the Nile below Khartoum. There is reason to believe that the river follows at this point the line of a diagonal fracture which is connected with the 'Gebel Elba breach' on the western rim of the Red Sea trough (Gregory, 1921, p. 351).

it comes so late in the series, it stands alone in the record as having added nothing to the physical sufferings of the Egyptians. It is a kind of portent, in fact, which we should expect an able writer to have invented as a *prelude* to the much heavier strokes that followed; a terrifying warning of what Egypt was to undergo if Jahweh's commands were disobeyed. That it has been left as it stands is therefore an encouraging sign of authenticity and when we examine it in detail this impression is very strongly confirmed.

> "*And Jahweh said unto Moses, Stretch out thine hand toward heaven, that there may be darkness over the land of Egypt, even darkness which may be felt. And Moses stretched forth his hand toward heaven; and there was a thick darkness in all the land of Egypt three days; they saw not one another, neither rose any from his place for three days.*"[1]

The usual explanation of this phenomenon is that it was 'occasioned really by a *sandstorm*, produced by the hot electrical wind called the *Ḥamsîn*, which in Egypt blows in most years intermittently—usually for two or three days at a time. . . . These winds . . . frequently raise such an amount of sand and dust as to darken the sun, and even to conceal objects a few yards off. . . . While the storm lasts, people are obliged to remain secluded in their houses. On account of the sand and dust the darkness is really such as "can be felt".'[2]

We have studied the miracles of the Exodus sufficiently by this time to realize that such a 'solution' of the problem

---

[1] Exod. x. 21–3. It is interesting to note that in Ps. cv the writer has actually transposed this plague, presumably for its greater artistic effect.

[2] Driver, *Exodus*, pp. 82–3. He cites such a storm '*c.* 1100, producing darkness so intense that it was thought the end of the world had come'.

carries its refutation upon its own surface. To any one who has lived for only a few years in the Near East the Ḥamsîn is an all too-familiar source of discomfort. It may be ranked indeed with the mosquito, the sand-fly, and the scorpion as one of those habitual pests which it is impossible to escape for long and which must be endured with the patience of long practice. To imagine such a phenomenon transformed into a portentous manifestation of Divine power is to see it through a haze which has entirely distorted its proportions. Whatever the Plague of Darkness was, it must have been something wholly abnormal, and when this fact is realized, the true explanation is not far to seek.

In the eruption of Vesuvius in 1906, the final phase was exactly of this character: 'The third or "dark ash" phase . . . began on April 9th, and lasted with constantly diminishing intensity for a fortnight. This consisted of the emission of gas clouds so charged with volcanic debris as to be quite black. At each emission an impenetrable pall of darkness covered Naples and the surrounding country. A hundred thousand people left the city, and religious processions, invoking the intercessions of the saints, filled the streets.'[1] Both in its physical features and in the superstitious awe which it inspired this pall of darkness vividly recalls its Egyptian counterpart, and it is significant that an account of a similar phenomenon in the Vesuvius eruption of 1822 actually contains the famous Biblical reference. The dust projected in vast clouds from the crater is described by an eyewitness[2] as having "filled the atmosphere, producing in the city of Naples 'a darkness that might be felt', and so excessively finely divided was it, that it penetrated into all drawers,

[1] Tyrrell, op. cit., p. 148.   [2] Judd, op. cit., p. 69.

boxes, and the most completely fastened receptacles, filling them completely".

Other examples may be added which will indicate the distances to which such a darkness may spread. In the Vesuvius eruption of 1717 there was intense darkness at 100 miles from the volcano. After the eruption of Tomboro in 1815 there was darkness for three days at a distance of 300 miles.[1] The eruption of eight volcanoes in the Andes in April 1932 threw a pall of darkness over practically the whole of the southern half of South America. The most stupendous, however, of all such phenomena was the thick sulphurous fog which extended over the whole of Europe to the north coast of Africa, Syria, and the Altai after the prodigious eruption of Skaptar Jökull (Iceland) in May–June 1783. Already before the end of May this fog had reached Copenhagen. It descended upon England in the middle of June and lasted there for two months. In some other parts it arrived later and stayed longer, no winds being able to disperse it. On July 9th it was described by a native of Peissenberg in Bavaria as being 'dense as an Egyptian plague'![2]

These facts may sound incredible to those who have not studied the phenomena of vulcanism. Actually it is almost impossible to over-estimate the forces which create these or the extent of the earth's surface over which they may make themselves felt. It is, for example, estimated that at the eruption of Krakatoa in 1883 some four cubic miles of dust were hurled into the air to wander three times round the earth in the upper atmosphere and create the gorgeous sunsets which our elders still remember. The heavier ashes fell on ships and islands

[1] *The Eruption of Krakatoa*, p. 393.   [2] Ib., pp. 388–92.

2,000 miles from the volcano. The sea-waves which wrecked the surrounding coast-villages were recorded strongly at Aden (3,380 miles), and definitely though less strongly at Port Elizabeth (4,690) and were even noted on the tidal charts at Devonport and Portland (considerably over 10,000 miles). In the Committee's report upon this eruption it was found necessary in the face of these facts to record the dictum that 'nothing can be said to be absolutely incredible in science until it has been proved to be absolutely impossible',[1] a warning which may serve to remind all students of the Old Testament that there are times when truth can be stranger than—folk-lore.

2. THE CATACLYSM OF THE RED SEA

We come, finally, to that crowning miracle of deliverance, the memory of which, if not more deeply rooted, has certainly been the most treasured of all the memories of Israel. Unfortunately it is this very fact which makes it difficult to disentangle the original story, for the text of the present record has been worked over by successive editors till it has become a mosaic of cunningly fitted fragments. We can, however, gather that the miracle was thought to have been performed by the Rod of God in the hand of Moses, and that

> "*the sea returned to its wonted flow when the morning appeared; and the Egyptians fled against it; and Jahweh shook off the Egyptians in the midst of the sea.*"[2]

The ascription of the phenomenon to the force of a 'strong east wind' which in the present text follows

[1] *The Eruption of Krakatoa*, p. 412.
[2] Exod. xiv. 27 (Mg): for the 'Rod of God' cf. Exod. iv. 17, 20; vii. 17, 20; xiv. 16.

immediately the mention of Moses' action, is in obvious conflict with the more primitive conception of the wonder-working Rod of God and must be accounted a devout rationalization.[1] A later generation reflecting upon this all-important crisis in Israel's history would appear to have supplied what it conceived to be the true cause of the miracle and in doing so to have brought about an effect the very opposite of that which it intended. For it would seem that this miracle needed no heightening of colour to lend it supernatural majesty, and Gressmann is undoubtedly on the right track when he refers it without hesitation to the result of a volcanic disturbance.[2] The phenomenon of the sea's recession followed by the onrush of a destructive tidal wave occurred at St. Pierre shortly before the great eruption of May 6th, 1902. After the mud-torrent of May 5th, the sea retreated 300 feet, overturning and grounding a yacht which was moored 500 feet from the shore. It then returned with great violence and threw the town into a momentary panic.[3] Tidal waves are, of course, frequently found in association with seismic and volcanic disturbances. The calamities of Messina and Reggio in 1908 are still a mournful memory. The explosion of some small volcanic islands in the Bismarck Archipelago in 1888 produced a similar effect on the neighbouring coast of New Pomerania.[4] In September 1538, when the great volcanic mass of Monte Nuovo came into being in the course of two days and nights, the sea off Pozzuoli suddenly retreated some 200 paces, leaving thousands of fishes high and dry on the beach. It then rushed back to the accompaniment of an earthquake and a violent

---

[1] Cf. Gressmann, *Mose*, p. 117. [2] Ib., p. 112 f.
[3] Heilprin, op. cit., p. 69. [4] Gressmann, *Mose*, p. 118.

volcanic eruption from the new crater.[1] Where Gressmann is less obviously correct in his reasoning is in his adoption of the Gulf of Akaba as the 'Sea' which was divided
before the passage of Israel.[2] By assuming this identification he gains the advantage of attributing the tidal wave
to the action of the Mount of God itself, since this *ex
hypothesi* stood at no great distance from the head of the gulf.
The theory is an attractive one; yet a consideration of the
circumstances seems to demand its rejection and to make
it more probable that the explosion of some volcanic
island or subterranean crater in the Red Sea itself was
the immediate cause of the catastrophe.

Against Gressmann's view must be urged the objection
that the Israelites could not possibly have covered the
whole distance between the Gulfs of Suez and Akaba
without being overtaken by the much swifter movements
of the Egyptian chariotry. If we are to suppose that they
had got thus far in safety, it must have been because there
was no pursuit at all. To produce the desired situation
of the Egyptians having just caught up with the fugitives
at this remote and critical point it would be necessary to
assume that the pursuit had not been launched till some
days, perhaps even a week, after the Exodus. But this is
unthinkable. If such a delay had occurred, the Egyptians
would have given up all hope of tracking down their
quarry, which would have vanished long since amongst
the wadis of the Tih plateau. Another defect of this
theory is that it does not provide the situation required
by the tradition. A crossing by the head of the Gulf of

[1] Gressmann, *Mose*, loc. cit.; Judd, op. cit., p. 76 f.

[2] Gressmann, *Mose*, p. 444. G. himself points out that in the present
recorded form of the Tradition the 'Sea' is nameless (p. 115): it is only
in later writers that it is definitely identified with the Yam Suph, i.e.
the Gulf of Akaba.

Suez, between the Red Sea (miraculously withdrawn) and the fortifications of the frontier to the north of it, supplies exactly that element of hopelessness and crisis which made the event so memorable. This the hypothesis of a crossing at the head of the Gulf of Akaba wholly fails to do. The pilgrim road through Nekl (the "*Way of the Wilderness of the Yam Suph*")[1] descends almost directly upon the present head of the gulf, while the Arabah to the north opposes no obstacle to the free passage of a multitude. For these reasons it seems best to adopt the commonly accepted view that the 'Sea' in question (and it is doubtful whether the oldest tradition knew it by a more definite name) was after all the Gulf of Suez, and that the miracle took place at some point near its head where no human being had ever seen dry ground.[2]

Then indeed we can picture a scene the memory of which may well have been indelible. We can discern in the darkness the dim masses of fugitive Israel hurrying in wonder across this beach so miraculously laid bare, while over against them the imprisoning wall of the frontier rose impotent, its might derided by the un-dreamed-of treachery of the sea. Some delay must have been inevitable before the pursuit of its garrison could be launched, for it calls for high courage to follow in the footsteps of despair: and when at last it pushed forward, Death with appalling speed raced down upon the horses and chariots and in a deluge of seething waters swept them away.

For Israel this awe-inspiring cataclysm stood out for ever as the greatest of the Egyptian signs and wonders;

[1] Exod. xiii. 18. See Map 2.

[2] On the extension of the Gulf northwards at this date, see above, p. 53, n. 1.

for the forces of which they had been hitherto the passive
spectators were exerted here at the most critical moment
of their escape. Upon this, then, all the rapture of their
thankfulness and elation was lavished: this was the mercy
which crowned for them the miracle of their deliverance,
and which they celebrated above all others in undying
strains of joy:

> *"Sing ye to Jahweh,*
> *For he hath triumphed gloriously;*
> *The horse and his rider*
> *hath he thrown into the sea."* [1]

Our task of reconstruction is now done, and it remains
only to gather the separate fragments into a connected
whole. It has been insisted throughout that neither the
faith of Israel nor its recorded history can be explained
satisfactorily without the assistance of 'miracles'. So far
this term has been used of the material phenomena
which effected so great a transformation in this People
and left behind them so deeply graven a memory, and
it is with these—still viewed as external and purely
mundane events—that we are at present concerned. A
miracle, as we have seen, must properly have two aspects:
there is the physical phenomenon which is said to have
occurred and there is the 'supernatural' explanation
which may be given of it. The second of these may, of
course, be quite erroneous, *but it would never have been given
at all if the first had not seemed to demand it.* We concluded,
then, that the phenomena to which the Israelite writers
bear witness must have been 'miracles' at least in the
looser and more popular sense of the word in that they

[1] Exod. xv. 21.

surpassed the normal experience of living men whether in power or in majesty or in both of these together. An examination of the only member of the series which has been scientifically investigated showed us at once the scale by which we must expect to measure the remainder and a clear indication as to their nature and origin. We are now in a position to claim that our expectations have been justified.

We find ourselves, then, in the presence of what must have been one of this earth's mightiest upheavals; a demonstration of its hidden forces so appalling in power and grandeur that the memory of it might well be in-effaceable. Over an area which must have covered thousands of miles the most stupendous convulsions of Nature known to man burst into sudden and violent activity, to play their part, often remote and invisible, in one of the greatest of all human stories. It must be a sluggish imagination which is not kindled by the picture which this thought evokes: actually it needs no imagina-tion at all to realize the effect which was wrought in the hearts of the Chosen People. For them, as these tremend-ous signs and wonders followed one another with tireless majesty, deeper and deeper the conviction was driven home that they had been called and delivered by a Power which was unique and utterly incomparable. No god in heaven or earth had ever stretched out his hand to work such marvels as these. But that was not all. To turn the greatest river in the world to blood and cover the mightiest kingdom on earth with darkness; to call back the heaving masses of the sea and release them in one terrific avalanche upon the enemy; to set up in the sky His towering beacon of cloud and flame; to descend upon His Holy Mountain in raging torrents of fire and lift up to His Chosen Leader the awful thunder of His Voice;—it was not merely that no god had done these things, it was much more that no god hitherto believed in and worshipped by Israel or its neighbours had been conceived of as possessing either the power or the will to do them. From that day, in one small corner of the earth, the very word GOD received, however unconsciously, a new meaning; for from that day out of the womb of awe and wonder and gratitude true Monotheism was destined to be born.

Chapter III

THE MIRACLE OF THE CALL

ON the summit of Plymouth Hoe stands a monument in memory of England's deliverance from the Armada which bears this brief inscription:

HE BLEW WITH HIS WINDS, AND THEY WERE SCATTERED.

These words and the fact to which they refer may be taken as a useful starting-point for a study of the deeper significance of Miracles.

About the facts themselves there is no dispute. At the end of July 1588, after a series of harassing engagements with the English fleet, the Armada turned northwards from the Flanders coast and attempted to return home by the route between Scotland and Norway. 'Up to this time the loss of the Spaniards in ships had not been considerable. If the weather had been that of a normal summer, they would probably have reached home with no greater loss of men than was usually inflicted on all fleets of the age by scurvy and fever. But the summer of 1588 was marked by a succession of gales of unprecedented violence. . . .'[1] The tragic end of the enterprise is well known. 'Of the total number of the vessels originally collected for the invasion of England one-half, if not more, perished, and the crews of those which escaped were terribly diminished by scurvy and starvation.' Yet far more important were the political effects of this disaster. 'It marked the final failure of King Philip II of Spain to establish the supremacy of the Habsburg

[1] *Enc. Brit.*, 11th ed., p. 560, s.v. 'Armada'.

dynasty and of the Church of Rome . . . in Europe. From that time forward no serious attempt to invade England was, or could be, made. It became, therefore, the unconquerable supporter of that part of Europe which had thrown off the authority of the Pope.'[1]

These are the facts objectively considered, and it is, of course, open to the student of history to leave them exactly as they stand. A particular physical phenomenon —a series of unprecedented gales—descends with sudden violence upon the fleet of the invader and not only ensures decisively the safety of England, but determines the whole course of European history.

But it is also open to the student to go beyond this bald review of mundane events. He may claim that for him they contain a far deeper significance and that unless they are interpreted on the level of Divine Purpose, their meaning must remain for ever unintelligible. For him, in other words, these gales are a Miracle in the strictest sense of the term: they were released upon the Armada even as the Red Sea was released upon the Egyptians; and it is with no shadow of hypocrisy that he can subscribe that verdict: *He blew with His winds, and they were scattered.*

Here then at last we reach the crux of our problem. Up to this point we have confined ourselves entirely to the objective study of the phenomena which Israelite Tradition records. We have been trying to discover *what really happened* without any reference to *why* it was believed to have happened; and just because these two questions are radically distinct, there is no argument in the preceding chapters with which a total agnostic might not agree. When we have spoken of the 'faith' of Israel, for example, we have not necessarily meant more by the term than

[1] Op. cit.

'a certain conviction of having been chosen by Jahweh which would not have existed if it had not rested ultimately on physical fact'. Even the materialist (if he exists) would accept such a definition without demur, for it is an obvious truth that no belief in God's Providence, however fallacious, could have come into being out of the empty air.

At the same time it should be noted that it is precisely here that our modern view of these Miracles diverges most widely from that of our forefathers. We no longer think of them as scientifically demonstrable proofs of Divine intervention, in which God, without making Himself actually visible to the eye, brought clearly (and sometimes even audibly) home to His Chosen People the meaning and purpose of His mighty works. We believe, on the contrary, that whoever had chanced to be present on the occasion of any of these great experiences of Israel would have seen and heard neither more nor less of the outward and visible phenomenon than the normal human senses are adapted, and able, to receive. We refuse, in other words, to except these particular experiences from the rules and conditions of ordinary life. That field is thrown open in its entirety to all observers; it has no secret corners to which the Elect alone are admitted: for all may see with their eyes and all may hear with their ears, but the deciding factor is whether they will understand.

We are facing now that mystery of faith and unbelief, of spiritual sight and blindness, which lies at the very heart of our religion. It is an undeniable fact, however we may try to explain it, that while there are some souls who seem to have a natural gift of spiritual percipience, there are numberless others to whom the attitude of faith is unintelligible and who can neither flog themselves nor be flogged by others into any kind of devotion to, or belief in, God. It is very commonly supposed to-day that this indifference is due to the increased complexity and interest of our secular preoccupations; and to a limited extent this is no doubt true. Certainly, with our greater knowledge of human frailty, we can discern more clearly than our fathers the obstacles which can make a religious faith virtually impossible: for we realize much more fully than they the inherent limitations of the individual human brain and its tendency to be dominated by forces of which it may be barely conscious. Innate prejudice, idiosyncrasy of character or temperament, inherited loyalties or traditions, physical environment, absorption in intellectual or mechanical pursuits, these are a few only of the barriers which can exclude the Heavenly Vision, and it may well be that with the increasing pressure of modern civilization, the number of such 'aids to blindness' is very greatly multiplied. Yet in going even thus far, it behoves us to be wary. Because we are only now becoming conscious of these 'various hindrances' to a living faith, we are apt to imagine that they are no more than a symptom of our age. But the mystery which we are pondering lies far below the transitory accidents of one phase in the history of mankind. It goes back, as it would seem, to some necessity which began with Man's creation, that there are some to whom "*it is given*" in this life to "*know the mysteries of the Kingdom of Heaven*", and others who, however rich their talents, in this respect remain poor.[1]

Here we are touching the paradox of Divine election, a theme far too vast to be pursued further in this place.

[1] Matt. xiii. 11. It is significant that Our Lord in His first parable dealt with this problem and gave this answer.

For the moment we must be content to face the facts which are obvious to any thoughtful observer of life and to realize what bearing they have upon our present subject. It must be clear at once that, given these two types of mind, the same natural phenomenon will be perceived by them in wholly different ways. To the one it will appear a subject for scientific investigation: to the other it may be (in addition to its scientific interest) a direct revelation of the Mercy or the Wrath of God. There is no Miracle, in other words, except to the eye that perceives it: we might add that to the eye which perceives it, it ceases in one sense to be a 'Miracle' at all. If this is not at first sight clear, a moment's reflection will show that it is really inevitable. To the eye of faith there can be no unnatural distinction between those events which may be termed 'miraculous' and those which may be classified as parts of our ordinary life. *"All things are of God . . . who worketh all things after the counsel of his will."* If that is true, there has been no moment in history, however tame or fleeting or insignificant, which has not been touched by that Hand or moulded to the working out of that Eternal Purpose. And that, indeed, is precisely what the experience of every faithful Christian has taught him. Times without number he has found his life (the life of one human being!) guided and decided and reshaped for him by incidents over which he has had little or no control: and he in his turn, when he offers his daily intercessions, believes that he has the power to be a fellow worker with God in building up and consecrating the lives of others.

Language like this is simply unintelligible to those who are spiritually blind. For them it is not the events called 'miracles' which are the real stumbling-block: it is the

N

daily, hourly, momentary miracle of the Providence of an Eternal Love. Actually it is far easier to accept that older view of miracles which saw the most High suddenly intervening in a world over which He had been exercising a more or less remote control than to credit the simple but staggering thought that one sparrow is not forgotten in the sight of God. That truth, so natural and obvious to the mind of a child, is the hardest of all sayings for a grown man who has learned something of the vastness of the universe. Immeasurably stupendous, it dwarfs into insignificance even the greatest of 'miraculous' phenomena; for it issues, so much more clearly than they, out of the very heart of the mystery of Eternity.

Where, then, in the realm of religious thought are we to place these miracles of the Exodus, and with what end in view should we study them? As overwhelming demonstrations of Providence which may be used for the conversion of the infidel they are now seen to be entirely valueless, since a man must already have *some* faith in God before he can acknowledge them to be the signs or instruments of His Will. But does this mean that they have lost all meaning or importance for Christians? It would be strange indeed if this were found to be so. For if the Scriptural interpretation of these phenomena is, as we believe, the true one, we may gain from them an insight such as is rarely given to man not only into the Counsels of God, but into the mode of His dealing with the souls who are to serve His Purpose.

His Purpose. That, after all, is what 'matters': not the old Israel, not ourselves, but that mystery of God's Will which He "*purposed . . . unto a dispensation of the fulness of the times, to sum up all things in Christ*".[1] It is that which

---

[1] Eph. i. 10.

makes both Books of the Bible one living inseparable whole; and it is only the deceptive familiarity of our unhappy translation 'Testament' which conceals from so many English readers the truth which their very titles proclaim. Old and New *Covenants*, Horeb and Calvary, both of them have one and the same story to tell, the story of a People sealed by the Blood of Sacrifice to serve the Royal Priesthood of their God:[1] and because the end of that story is not yet written, because we, as we live, are by God's grace helping to write it, these records of Holy Scripture which reveal the plan and method of its Author are for us the most precious documents upon earth. On such a view it is not difficult to determine the place which these Miracles of the Exodus must hold in the hearts of Christians; for it was through them that there came into being the People "*of whom is Christ as concerning the flesh*". How great an office that was which they performed is a thought which we may do well to ponder, reminding ourselves that the assurance of His physical descent was perhaps the smallest part of it. The undying trust in God's love for His Chosen People; the stern demand for thankful obedience to His Will; the vision of His Holiness, no less than of His Power and Majesty—all these were needed to consummate that far-off "*fulness of the times*". As we look back, indeed, upon the vicissitudes of Israel's history, the fury and the flush of conquest, the pride of sovereignty and its undoing, captivity, exile, and that last tragedy of disappointment from which the figure of a Suffering Servant rises for a moment like a false dawn of Easter, we can learn what measure of harvest had to be sown and gathered, before there could be prepared a homeland and a mother for the Incarnate Son of God.

[1] Exod. xix. 5–6; 1 Pet. ii. 9.

All that is implied in those words 'the Faith of Israel' lies in that background, in that ploughed and furrowed soil; and it was here, in the signs and wonders of Egypt, Horeb, and Jordan, that the seed of that harvest was sown.

If, then, we still retain for these phenomena their ancient title of Miracle, it is to claim for them a wonder not less but infinitely greater than that which our fore-fathers could have confessed. Not from the Heavens was the Call of Israel sounded: no Voice, sublime and terrible, proclaimed its destiny in words that all might compre-hend: only through the course of the ages the Earth's slow travail moved towards this moment, when this message might be uttered in the ears which could alone receive it, and this act accomplished on those for whom it was ordained. Surely, there is here a Miracle indeed; a revelation of Power and Wisdom, awful not least for its calm and vast simplicity: a Miracle of Coincidence, as we may call it, not single but threefold, in which matter and spirit meet together in marvellous conjunction.

There is, first, what may be termed the Miracle of Material Coincidence; the impact of purely external phenomena upon the normal human senses of Israel and its enemies. On this we need not linger, for the part which it played is already sufficiently clear. It is enough to state the fact (if the reader will now concede it to be such) that at that particular time on that particular area of the earth's surface there was manifested a series of stupendous phenomena, capable (and more than capable) of delivering this particular people from hopeless slavery, of forging them into a Nation, and of leading them in triumph to the land which was to be their home.

There is, secondly, the Miracle of Coincidence which we may distinguish for our present purpose as Spiritual;

the presence, at that critical moment in the midst of Israel, of one who may justly be called its master-soul. We need not repeat here what has already been said of the spiritual eminence of Moses.[1] It is enough to point out that it is the sheer necessity of the facts which constrains us to this conclusion: that here was one not only of earth's noblest leaders but of the greatest of the saints of God. Indeed, if we may slightly anticipate our argument, the story of his Call from the Burning Bush would alone suggest this probability; for such an experience seems never to be granted to a human soul, unless that soul is fitted for the highest service of the Master. Then when the refining fires of tribulation and penitence have done their work, and the grossness of pride and self-confidence has been purged away, the Call comes clearly through the channel of some earthly instrument and sets that soul ablaze. So it was that it came to St. Augustine, out of the lips of a romping child. So it was with St. Francis, kneeling at the Mass in St. Mary of the Angels. So (need we doubt it?) it was with Moses in the darkest hour of his disappointment and despair. Without that story, it is true, we should still have been forced to assume his greatness: with it, the whole course of events is amply and admirably clarified. He stands before us in that crisis as one who has scaled the heights; as one who through stern discipline has received the crown of enlightenment, and with it the fullest power to mediate to his countrymen the glory and the mystery of their God.

We have already drawn attention to the fact that the Faith of Israel presupposed the existence of such a man as one of the necessary factors which brought it into being. So much, indeed, must be assumed from a purely

[1] See above, p. 42.

psychological standpoint, if the history of this people is not to remain a complete enigma. But here we are concerned with a profounder view of life, and it is on this level that we recognize the true significance of Moses. We have spoken by anticipation of his 'Call' from God, and we must face now what that word involves. We shall not necessarily find it easy to do so. We are so familiar with the idea of God's Sovereignty over 'Nature' that we may experience no great difficulty in accepting what have been termed above the Miracles of Material Coincidence. But it is quite otherwise with those which display His equal Sovereignty over the births, the lives, and the deaths of men and women. Whatever lip-service we may pay to the claims of the Divine Potter, we are most of us stubbornly reluctant to regard ourselves as His clay; and we shrink from a view of the Universe which would weave our personal destinies into the common texture of all created things. We may need, then, to confess in ourselves this failure of self-abasement, if we are to study aright the Call both of this Nation and of this Man. Only so can we approach the marvel of that ordained fulfilment, that such a servant should "*come to the kingdom for such a time*".[1]

Lastly, there is that which, for lack of a better term, we must be content to call the Miracle of Sacramental Coincidence; the fact, namely, that there was in the nature of the phenomena themselves a reservoir of inexhaustible spiritual significance. Without this, indeed, the efforts of Moses would have been useless, for it was his task not to create a new religion out of his own brain but to interpret by his spirit the things which he saw and heard; yet it may be doubted if the full wonder of these

[1] Esther iv. 14.

experiences was realized even by Moses as it was felt and proclaimed by the faithful souls who followed him. For them, as we have seen, the essential meaning of these facts remained unaltered—The Call of the Chosen People; its triumphant Deliverance from Egypt; the solemn Covenant of Election sealed in the flames and thunders of the Mount of God—these for all later generations of Israelites were at once the charter of the Nation's destiny and the sanctions of its Faith. Yet this, as they came to see, was not all that these signs and wonders held in their secret depths. There was a vision of infinite Power and sovereign Majesty which towered ever more clearly over the horizon of the whole world. There was a splendour of awful Holiness dwelling in fires more terrible than those of Horeb. There was a mystery of cloud and thick darkness which veiled eternally the invisible and formless King. Most wonderful of all, there was the revelation of a Love, free and abounding, of which not Israel only might learn, and share, the grace. . . .

The age, the moment, the place, the people, the man —as we contemplate this mighty fashioning together of time and matter and space and spirit, we perceive with deepening awe how the pattern which it traces blends ever more clearly through the centuries into the lineaments of a living Face; till, in the fullness of the times, that Face itself rises before us, marred yet most lovely; and we worship Him in whom all Miracles are fulfilled.

> *"When Israel was a child, then I loved him*
> *And called my son out of Egypt."*

These simple words of Hosea must always ring as challenge to the faith of the New Israel. What part in all this might not self-deception have played? Was Moses himself no more than the dupe of those terrific forces of Nature which seemed to his naïve religious consciousness so clearly exerted for the benefit of his countrymen? Is this after all the explanation of that stupendous experience in which the People of whom is Christ as concerning the flesh found against all hope and expectation their freedom, their destiny, and their God?

Shall we give place to these doubts and set this story aside? Or shall we, for whom all history is an unfolding of God's Purpose, fix our eyes rather with the greater intentness upon those moments in it when that Purpose comes nearest to open vision on this earth; when the Power and the Wisdom of that unresting Energy seem focused with supreme intensity upon one point in space and time? For Christians there is no need to pause for an answer. For whether this revelation of Redeeming Love bursts into the humble routine of our lives, or whether we view it across the gulf of centuries as it forges a nation for the Incarnate Saviour of the World, we may feel in our hearts the fire that exalts and transfigures, the light that illumines the panorama of transitory things: and there falls upon us the glory of the Transcendent Godhead, weaving His counsels indefectibly through the strivings and the sins of men:

> O THE DEPTH OF THE RICHES BOTH OF THE WISDOM AND THE KNOWLEDGE OF GOD! HOW UNSEARCHABLE ARE HIS JUDGEMENTS, AND HIS WAYS PAST TRACING OUT! FOR WHO HATH KNOWN THE MIND OF THE LORD? OR WHO HATH BEEN HIS COUNSELLOR? OR WHO HATH FIRST GIVEN TO HIM, AND IT SHALL BE RECOMPENSED UNTO HIM AGAIN? FOR OF HIM, AND THROUGH HIM, AND UNTO HIM, ARE ALL THINGS. TO HIM BE THE GLORY FOR EVER. AMEN.

APPENDIXES

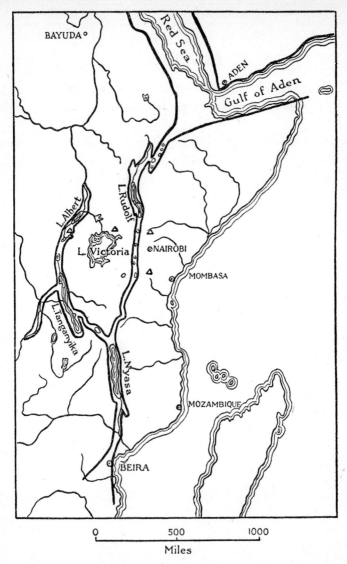

THE RIFT VALLEYS OF EAST AND CENTRAL AFRICA

From *Inland Waters of Africa*, by S. and E. B. Worthington,
by permission of Macmillan & Co., Ltd.

Appendix I

THE ARABAH AND KADESH-BARNEA

The deep rift of the Arabah which links the Dead Sea with the Gulf of Akaba enters the full light of Biblical history for the first time in the reign of Solomon.

> "*And king Solomon made a navy of ships in Ezion-geber which is beside Eloth, on the shore of the Yam Suph, in the land of Edom.*"[1]

It is true that this harbour lies at the southernmost extremity of the rift and that it would have been possible for the Israelite caravans to have avoided the passage through it on their way to and from Jerusalem; yet there are indications that at one period at least the whole extent of the Arabah was in Israelite hands, and the indirect inferences which may be drawn from this are of considerable interest to the student of Israelite tradition.

1. The exact location of the port of Ezion-geber may be regarded as known. It is to be found not at Ain Ghadian[2] but at el-Meniyyeh, about fifteen miles from the head of the gulf. The place has been described by Dr. Musil, who visited it in 1902. The guide told him that a town had once stood on the *wadi* of that name, the inhabitants of which possessed a very large navy. They had, however, offended Allah and, as a result, there descended a long and torrential downpour of rain which choked with boulders not only the *wadi* but the gulf itself, destroying the city and causing the Red Sea to retreat to its present level.[3] There seems

---

[1] 1 Kings ix. 26.

[2] 'Solomon's great seaport must surely have measured more than fifty yards each way, and it would strain the Indian Ocean to bring it two hundred feet uphill.' *P.E.F. Annual*, 1914–15, p. 13. El-Meniyyeh is about 10 miles from the present head of the gulf, an arm of which seems once to have reached it. [3] A. Musil, *Edom*, Vienna, 1908, ii, p. 187.

to be a reasonably clear reminiscence in this story of how the ships of Jehoshaphat were "*broken at Ezion-Geber*"[1] and the port transferred by Uzziah to Elath or Eloth, near the modern Akaba.[2] Mr. George Horsfield, who recently visited el-Meniyyeh, has informed the present writer that the remains of a citadel are clearly visible there and that, in addition to this, the *wadi* contains the remains of slag-heaps such as are to be found at the northern end of the Arabah at the copper-workings of el-Nahas and Fenan. The pottery fragments observed by him seemed to belong to the Middle Bronze Age, but this of course means only that the Israelite depot still remains to be located. In any case, on our knowledge of the facts, it may be assumed without great daring that some at least of these traces of a mining industry were associated with the Ophir expeditions of Solomon and that, in fact, the copper resources of the Arabah were traded by his merchants for the gold and ivory of less civilized lands.

It may be pointed out, in passing, that some such hypothesis as this is in any case desiderated, if we are to account satisfactorily for the wealth amassed by Solomon. Even if the traditional accounts of it are grossly exaggerated, they cannot be wholly without substance and it cannot be said that so far they have been adequately explained. Palestine itself possesses no mineral resources and its agricultural produce though carefully organized was barely sufficient for the needs of the king's court.[3] It has been suggested that Solomon 'made his money' by acting as middleman between Egypt and the Hittite and Aramaean kingdoms, and that he enriched himself further by taxing heavily the Arabian spice-caravans which passed through his territory. All this may be true up to a point, yet the hard law of economics— that you cannot get something for nothing—obliges us to look elsewhere for the substantial basis of his wealth. His famous expeditions from Ezion-geber must have carried

---

[1] 1 Kings xxii. 48.   [2] 2 Kings xiv. 22.   [3] 1 Kings iv. 7–19.

with them *something* valuable which they could use for barter, and it would seem reasonable to suppose that this 'something' included at least the copper-ore of the Arabah, whether 'in the raw' or in the form of manufactured articles. Nor was this the only use to which Solomon could put the metal. A vast quantity of it was also needed for the temple vessels and we are told that these were cast in the Jordan Valley 'in the clay-ground between Succoth and Zarethan'.[1] The choice of site may have been due to the proximity of the rich wood-supply which the forests of Gilead afforded, but if the copper itself was mined at Fenan (Punon) and el-Nahas and transported thence by way of the Dead Sea, the Jordan Valley was obviously the most convenient place in which the casting could be carried out. Gilead itself, though it shows traces of ancient iron-working, has so far revealed no signs of copper, so that we are precluded from seeking the origin of the metal from thence.

If this argument is allowed a certain plausibility, it may be permitted to develop itself further. For the possession of the copper-mines of the Arabah by Israel certain indispensable preliminaries had to be performed. In other words, the approaches to the Arabah had to be secured by pacific or belligerent means and the inhabitants of the actual sites and their environment had to be reduced to submission. To put it more briefly, the Amalekites, the Kenites, and the Edomites had first to be dealt with. But these people come first into view with the campaigns of Saul and his successor David, and the suspicion very naturally arises that the value of the copper-mines of the Arabah was well known to Israel even before the reign of Solomon. Is it not, in fact, possible that the whole trend of Israelite strategy from the days of the Philistine oppression onwards was to obtain possession of this rift-valley which contained the only mineral resources within reasonable reach? We may go further. The legendary friendship of the Kenites and

----

[1] 1 Kings vii. 46.

Israelites immediately after the Exodus may or may not
have an historical basis: this will be considered below. What,
however, seems to be quite certain is that the legend itself
would never have survived at all unless the Kenites had
been at *some* historical period in a position to help or to
hinder the interests of Israel. The word Keni or Kenite
means 'smith' in Aramaic, and it was long ago suggested
by Sayce that the people who bore it were travelling metal-
workers who may have provided Israel with the weapons
which the Philistines denied them.[1] This view has been
recently doubted,[2] but it would be considerably reinforced
if it could be shown that the Kenites were not merely copper-
smiths but *actually possessors* of the districts from which the
metal was mined. Although parties of them seem to have
moved up into the Negeb and even found their way into
the plain of Esdraelon, their connexion with the Edomite
clan of Kenaz[3] indicates what must have been their real
homeland. This is borne out by the punning 'proverb' of
Num. xxiv. 21, which has been converted into a prophecy
and put into the mouth of Balaam. If we examine this
verse closely, we find that it yields precise and important
information. Its date, to begin with, may be assigned to the
last years of the reign of Saul, since the association of the
Kenites with the Amalekites in Num. xxiv. 20–1 has its
historical counterpart in that period only (1 Sam. xv. 6).
The annihilation of Amalek is, in fact, celebrated in the
preceding verse, not as a prophecy (though it is capable by
its vagueness of being treated as one and, as it stands in its
present context, has this meaning forced upon it) but as an
historical event which is hailed with savage jubilation:

"*First of nations* [is or was] *Amalek but his last* [is or was]
unto destruction".

This is simply an ironic word-play upon what must have

[1] *H.D.B.* ii. 834, s.v. 'Kenites'.
[2] Cf. Lods, *Israel*, 1932, pp. 205–6, 318.   [3] Gen. xv. 19.

been a well-known Amalekite boast: it is a taunt, the very
zest of which is hot with the flush of victory. When we turn
to the 'proverb' upon the Kenites which is closely linked
with it, we find, *mutatis mutandis*, a marked resemblance.
While the tone here is, as might be expected, friendly, there
is the same punning humour as in the saying on Amalek;
and, if we ignore the concluding couplet which seems to have
been added at a much later date (cf. the reference to Asshur)
to turn it into a prophecy, the same terse and pithy compres-
sion. Translated literally the verse runs:

> "*Everflowing* [*is*] *thy habitation*
> *And set in the crag* (Sela) *thy Nest* (Ken)."

The point of the 'proverb' is, of course, quite clear: it is to
congratulate the Kenites on certain peculiar excellences of
their stronghold. The pun on Ken and Kenite in the second
line is equally obvious, but what is the meaning of the riddle
in the first? The usual answer is to deny that there is a
riddle at all and to assume that the word איתן is to be understood metaphorically and translated 'strong' or 'ever-
during'. But this is surely to miss the whole spirit of the
'proverb', every term in which must be meant to be taken
literally. Now the literal meaning of איתן 'ever-flowing' has
a very real significance for Palestinians to whom the possession of a perennial spring is a treasure to be highly prized.
Such a stream was even regarded as specially sacrosanct,[1]
and the prophet Amos sees in it a fit simile for that continual
outpouring of righteousness which Jahweh desires from His
people.[2] It may be assumed then, that the Kenite stronghold was distinguished in some marked manner by the
character of its ever-flowing water-supply, while it also
possessed a citadel perched (we may suppose impregnably)
on a crag (Sela). The old identification of the Edomite
Sela with Petra rushes at this point irresistibly into the mind,
and it may be said, by anticipation, that all the evidence

[1] Deut. xxi. 4.   [2] Amos v. 24.

seems in its favour. Here it must suffice to point out how exactly the Kenite proverb fits the site. In Petra we have, on the one hand, a 'habitation' the whole character of which has been created and determined by its ever-flowing stream, and, on the other, in the heart of this extraordinary city, an impregnable citadel perched like an eagle's nest on a bare crag and defended on all sides by lofty precipices.[1] We have, in short, not merely a locality which entirely satisfies the description, but one whose very peculiarities lend themselves most readily to this type of riddling proverb.

The identification of the old Kenite stronghold with the Edomite Sela, and of Sela with Petra, may go far to explain the importance of the Kenite alliance for Israel during the reigns of David and Solomon. A glance at the map will show that Petra is the key-position of the entire Arabah. It dominates both the copper-mine area of el-Nahas and Fenan to the north and the approaches to the Gulf of Akaba on the south. With the inhabitants of this stronghold not merely neutral, but friendly, the chief obstacle to the ambitions of Israel was removed. It remained, in fact, only to subjugate the remainder of Edom, and this was carried out under David's orders with a ferocity which would be unintelligible if the end in view had been simply political domination.[2] It is interesting to notice how in some respects the history of Israel's struggles for the Arabah tended to repeat itself. The first decisive victory over Edom was won by David or by Abishai in the Valley of Salt,[3] which may be the present el-Sebha at the south end of the Dead Sea. If, as we are assuming, Sela was in friendly hands, the way then lay open to the gulf. Certainly the establishment by Solomon of his port at Ezion-geber seems to have followed

[1] The old citadel of Petra is called to-day el-Biyara. Its summit lies over 3,000 feet above the level of the Wadi Musa. It is completely isolated and accessible only by rock-cut steps.

[2] 2 Sam. viii. 13; 1 Kings xi. 15.

[3] 2 Sam. viii. 13; 1 Chron. xviii. 12.

without further fighting in the Arabah. A century later Israel was not so fortunate. In the reign of Jehoram Edom successfully revolted, and the Arabah was lost. It was recovered temporarily by Amaziah who won, like David, a great victory in the Valley of Salt, but was forced in addition to capture Sela,[1] which this time was in enemy hands. This was apparently the first, as it was certainly the last, time that Petra was an Israelite possession, and the achievement was duly celebrated by Amaziah, who gave it the new name of Joktheel. The fruits of his able generalship were gathered by his son Uzziah, precisely as those of David's Edomite wars were reaped by Solomon. But Ezion-geber had long since ceased to exist as a harbour, and the new port on the Gulf of Akaba was established at Elath. It was a short-lived venture, for Elath was regained by the Edomites in the reign of Uzziah's grandson,[2] and Judah was never again strong enough to challenge its ancient enemy. Yet it remains a remarkable fact that for two periods in its history, from David to Jehoshaphat, and again from Uzziah to Ahaz, the Arabah was in the hands of Israel, and might even be reckoned as Israelite territory.

2. But *was* it actually so reckoned? There is evidence that it was. First, there is the curious and apparently baseless reference in Deuteronomy to certain hills in the Land of Promise from which Israel would be able to 'dig brass'.[3] Now it appears to be certain that no part of the Israelite territory proper contained this ore, so that the 'prophecy' must refer to the mines of the Arabah. It must, in fact, have been well known both to the writer and to his readers that at some period Israel was in possession of these copper mines, and it must, further, have been possible to allude to them *as lying within the borders of the Nation's territory.* In other words, it must have been possible to claim the Arabah as belonging to Israel, and to exclude it, in consequence, from the territory of Edom. Theoretically, it is by no means difficult to

[1] 2 Kings xiv. 7.   [2] 2 Kings xvi. 6.   [3] Deut. viii. 9.

do this. With the exception of Petra itself, the chief towns of Edom lay high up either on the summit of the great limestone plateau or on the lofty spurs which jut out from it towards the west. If a line be roughly drawn southwards from the south-east end of the Dead Sea, through el-Nahas, Fenan, and Petra to Akaba, it will be found that no ancient Edomite settlement of any importance is left to the west of it. But we are not confined to theory. In Judges i. 36, the border of the Edomites[1] is laid down along this very line! It was 'from the ascent of Akrabbim from the crag (Sela) and upwards'. The ascent of Akrabbim has been identified with various routes on the west edge of the Arabah, in spite of the fact that it still exists under the same name to-day near the south-east end of the Lisan! At a point where a very ancient road climbs tortuously up from the shores of the Dead Sea to the village of Kethrabbe there lie the ruins of Umm el-Akareb. The name means 'scorpion' in both Hebrew and Arabic, and the identity of the two is hardly open to dispute.[2] The other extremity of this line is at Sela (Petra) itself and it is stated that everything 'upward', i.e. eastwards up the slopes of the plateau between these two points, belonged to Edom, the unwritten but obvious inference being, of course, that everything 'downwards', or westwards, from it belonged to Israel.

But this is by no means all. The southern border of Israel (as laid down in Num. xxxiv. 3 ff.) follows the same line:

> "*Your south quarter [corner] shall be from the wilderness of Zin along by the side of Edom, and your south border shall be from the end of the Salt Sea eastward: and your border shall turn about southward of the ascent of Akrabbim, and pass along to Zin:*

[1] Cf. Burney, *Judges*, p. 33, note. The reading 'Amorites' is unintelligible.

[2] That the border started so far to the north of the present south-east end of the Dead Sea is probably due to the fact that the southern basin of the Sea has been slowly encroaching upon its shores. Cf. Albright, *The Archaeology of Palestine and the Bible*, p. 135.

*and the goings out thereof shall be southward of Kadesh-barnea;
and it shall go forth to Hazar-addar, and pass along to Azmon:
and the border shall turn about from Azmon unto the brook of
Egypt, and the goings out thereof shall be at the sea."*

(The description of the south border of Judah in Joshua xv.
3 ff., follows this account closely, but it substitutes Hezron
and Addar (two places) for Hazar-Addar, and appears in
some respects to be later and less reliable.)

With the help of the clue given in Judges i. 36, it is not
difficult to give this description a very real precision. It
starts with the general proposition that the south border of
Israel was not one which ran simply from east to west, but
formed a 'corner', one side of which went 'along by the side
of Edom'. Actually, it began at the end of the Salt Sea and
ran *eastward* to the ascent of Akrabbim. There it 'turned
about' [ran southwards] to Kadesh-barnea through the
wilderness or pasture land of Zin. Thence it 'went forth'
[i.e. there was some change of direction] to Hazar-Addar,
'passed along' [went direct] to Azmon, and 'turned about'
[swung north] from there to the brook of Egypt, which it
followed to the Mediterranean. The double place-name
Hazar-Addar is unknown, but as the form Hezron appears
in the parallel passage in Joshua, it is not impossible that
the original reading was Ezion-geber, which became cor-
rupted when the port went out of existence and its name
ceased to be familiar. Be this as it may, the line of the border
'along by the side of Edom' is very obviously the same as that
described in Judges, and as there is no other important point
on it but Petra, it seems to follow that we must accept the
equation Sela = Petra = Kadesh-barnea.

The time would seem to be ripe for reopening the old and
much-debated problem which centres round this last name.[1]

[1] Musil (*N.H.*, Appendix V) places Kadesh-barnea in the neighbourhood of Petra, but his treatment of the documentary evidence is un-
critical and his arrival at this conclusion would appear to be
fortuitous.

As a matter of fact there is in a sense no need to reopen it, for the question reopened itself almost automatically from the moment when it was found that Trumbull's exuberant description of Ain Kadeis was not merely over-coloured but wholly imaginative, and that the name Kadeis has nothing whatsoever to do with 'holiness', but denotes 'a wooden scoop or bailer used for lifting water from a shallow well'![1] After this it is really quite useless to resort to the desperate expedient of shifting the original 'Kadesh' to the more fertile Ain Guderat in its neighbourhood simply because that spring seems more fitted to represent it. It is wiser to face the truth, and the truth is that we have not one particle of evidence that there ever was any spring called 'Holy' in the Negeb at all. We are back precisely where we were before Rowlands's fateful discovery of Ain Kadeis:[2] in other words, we are back in the Arabah. No one before Rowlands made any serious effort to look for Kadesh-barnea elsewhere, and there was no reason why anybody should. The Biblical evidence, when dispassionately examined, points too clearly in that direction to leave room for serious doubt. We have only to consider the list of halting-places in Num. xxxiii. 36–44 to see that this is conclusive as far at least as Solomonic tradition is concerned. The stations in question are apparently laid out as leading, perhaps in a roundabout way, from somewhere in the Sinai Peninsula.[3] The earlier stations

---

[1] *P.E.F. Annual*, 1914–15, p. 53 f.

[2] Trumbull, *Kadesh-barnea*, pp. 211 ff.

[3] As has been suggested above, it is possible that Solomon may have attempted to work the copper and turquoise mines there as well as the mines in the Arabah. In 1 Kings ix. 18 he is said to have built 'Baalath and Tamar in the wilderness in the land'. The last words are quite meaningless, and Böttcher proposed by a simple emendation to read 'in the wilderness of Paran'; cf. Burney, *Notes on Hebrew Text of the Book of Kings*, 1903, p. 138. If Paran is Feiran, then Tamar may be the modern port of Tor, and Baalath the famous inland mining-camp of the Lady of the Turquoise, the 'Baalat' of the Sinaitic inscriptions. If the reading of Seirite names in these is correct, the connexion

(after Sinai) are all of them unknown: in verse 36, however, we find Ezion-geber (which dates the list since this port was replaced by Elath after the disaster in the reign of Jehosha-phat) the next station to which is 'the wilderness of Zin (the same is Kadesh)'. After this comes Mount Hor 'in the edge of the land of Edom'; then an unknown Zalmonah; then Punon (Fenan); then Oboth (unknown); then Iye-abarim 'in the border of Moab'. The route is conceived, in other words, as descending into the Arabah at Ezion-geber (el-Meniyyeh) and then making north-eastwards across it towards the 'border of Moab' by way of the 'edge of Edom'. If, as we have supposed, the 'wilderness' of Zin was the region lying round Fenan and el-Nahas, then Kadesh, which is regarded as identical with it, must be close at hand. But we have already seen that Kadesh can be equated with Sela-Petra, or rather perhaps with its high places, and we have suggested that the old Israelite border may have crossed the Arabah from Sela to Ezion-geber. The two lines of argument seem therefore to converge, and here we may join them with a third.

The most extraordinary feature of Petra is the famous Sîk, a narrow chasm, in places not more than 12 feet wide, which running for a mile and a half between lofty precipi-tous cliffs carries in its bed the waters of Ain Musa. Such a place must from the first have boasted a legendary origin. Indeed we may conjecture that before it became known to the Israelites this gorge was believed to have been made in the course of a fierce struggle between demons or demi-gods, in which one of these gigantic combatants had rent the solid rock with the fury of his blow: ever thereafter the

between the two mining areas may date back to very ancient times. The knowledge of the Sinai mines would certainly be available to Solomon, for the last Pharaoh to work them was Rameses IV (c. 1160). It is a point worth considering whether the Mosaic traditions of the peninsula may not have arisen first, with those of Petra, during the 'Augustan Age' of Solomon and his immediate successors, and from the same cause.

waters which flowed through it retained the memory of this feat: they were the waters of Meribah—the Waters of Strife. To Israel, on the other hand, a very different explanation presented itself. Surely it was here (whether for the first or second time) that Moses brought water from the rock by the wonder-working power of the Rod of God! The very depth of the chasm proclaimed the superhuman force behind that stroke and the wrath with which the Leader had carried out Jahweh's commands. As for the old name Meribah this must certainly be accounted for by some incident in the same story. Either God 'strove' with Levi or it was the People who 'strove' with Moses or with Jahweh Himself: this was of secondary importance and could be left to the popular imagination.[1] From that day onwards— and we cannot exclude the possibility of a date so early as even the reign of Solomon—the site of Kadesh-barnea would be regarded as definitely identified. Rabbinical writers, following no doubt the 'priestly' redaction, make this assumption as a matter of course. For them Kadesh is Rekem or Rekem-giah, another name for Petra, and Josephus, followed by Eusebius and Jerome, accepts the same conclusion.[2] The modern names Ain and Wadi Musa thus perpetuate a tradition which must date back at the latest to post-exilic Jewry, but which is very probably (in germ at least) many centuries older.

In what *order* did this legend arise? Was the water-miracle attached to an already existing Kadesh when the strange appearance of the Sîk was first noted by Israelite visitors to Sela? Or, on the other hand, was Sela identified with Kadesh because the tradition already connected a water-miracle with a Kadesh and, as it were, forced that name upon the Kenite stronghold? The answer would seem to be clear; for, firstly, Kadesh-barnea is mentioned in Deuter-

---

[1] See above, p. 70. This uncertainty is itself a clear indication of the pre-Israelite origin of the name Meribah.

[2] Trumbull, *Kadesh-barnea*, p. 167 f.

onomy and deuteronomic redactions without any suggestion
that it was the place at which the rock was made to bring
forth water, and secondly (as we have seen from our analysis
of the documents), the original tradition connected the
miracle not with Kadesh at all but with the Midianite
Horeb.[1] It must be inferred therefore that the oldest name
of the high place of Sela was Kadesh-barnea, while the
'ever-flowing' stream of the Wadi Musa was known as the
'Waters of Meribah of Kadesh', and that it was solely owing
to the abnormal appearance of the Sîk that a *second* water-
miracle was postulated at this later stage of the wanderings
of Israel.

It will follow also, at the least as a possibility, that the
tradition of Israel's sojourn at Kadesh-barnea is an authentic memory of the facts. From Horeb in southern Midian
the People would have marched towards Palestine by the
'Mount Seir road',[2] and the first most obvious halting-place
would have been Sela-Petra. From here they would
naturally make their assault upon the Negeb—that ascent
of the Mount of the Amorites (i.e. the western edge of the
Arabah) which ended so disastrously. Chased back down
the slopes as far as Hormah (the present Kornub?) they
retired to their base across the valley and gave up all hope
of invading Canaan from the south.[3]

Yet their stay at Kadesh-barnea had not been altogether
fruitless, for it must have been here that they made alliance
not only with the Kenites whose friendship was to be of such
value in later years, but also with the Kenizzite clan of Caleb
through whose prowess the strongholds of Hebron and Debir
came ultimately into the possession of Judah.[4] Whether the
Kenizzite invasion was a more successful repetition of the old
Israelite effort against the Negeb is a matter for speculation
which in the absence of any kind of evidence is necessarily

[1] See above, p. 71.   [2] Deut. i. 2.
[3] Num. xiv. 45; Deut. i. 19, 44.
[4] Joshua xv. 14–17; Judges i. 10–13.

futile. The Israelite writers themselves are silent, for the only invasion of Canaan which interests them is that which was launched against Jericho and they only record in the briefest terms the vengeance which finally overtook the kings of Arad and Hormah.[1]

[1] Num. xxi. 1–3.

Appendix II

THE BOUNDARIES AND TOPOGRAPHY OF MIDIAN

1. *The Boundaries.* Opinions differ very widely as to the exact boundaries and extent of this famous Bedouin tribe, but this is not to say that we are left entirely to conjecture. Even to-day the limits of tribal territories are laid down with remarkable clearness, as the traveller knows to his cost when, on crossing from one such area to another, he finds it necessary to secure new guides and protectors through the district into which he has intruded. Even in comparatively featureless tracts these tribal boundaries are well observed; but a striking physical line of division will naturally increase their rigidity. Such a line is laid down by nature along the great rift of the Arabah. Here, with the great mountain chain which crowns its eastern border, it presents to the western desert of Arabia Petraea a forbidding barrier which the Bedouin of all times have been slow to cross. Those in the Negeb of Palestine and in the peninsula to the south of it have thus been naturally separated from their brethren of the east, and these, in turn, rather than brave the fierce heat of the waterless Arabah and its arduous descents, have found their lines of expansion and intercourse along the great routes which lead northward to Damascus, southward to Medina and the distant Yemen, and eastward to the great oases of Jauf, Hail, and Riad.

It is to the second of these groups that the Midianites clearly belonged, and not to the western tribes, which were known to Israel as the Amalekites. The name of Midian in early genealogies is connected with the famous eastern tribes of Sheba and Dedan;[1] and these again are linked, both by

[1] Gen. xxv. 1–3; Isa. lx. 6.

trade and race, with Cushite East Africa, the modern Somaliland, Abyssinia, and the northern Sudan.[1] Sheba itself is closely connected with the oasis of Tema[2] (modern Teima, 150 miles ESE. of Tebuk), while Dedan has been rediscovered at el-'Ala (75 miles SW. of Teima).[3] Both these places lie on or near the northern caravan routes from Medina and east of the lava-fields of the Northern Hejaz. The Midianite clan-name Ephah has been recognized as surviving in the modern Rwafa on the western edge of the same volcanic regions;[4] and a 'city of Madian', with its surrounding district of the same name, was well known to Roman and Arab geographers as situated on the east coast of the Gulf of Akaba. We need, in fact, have no hesitation in identifying this city with the oasis of Beda (Beida el-Haura) which lies at the foot of the great coastal range, five days' march from Aila (near Akaba) and six days from Tebuk, as calculated by the ancient travellers.[5] At first sight this identification of Beda with the city of Midian precludes the necessity for a further search: somewhere, it would appear certain, in the neighbourhood of this oasis must be found the Mount of God.[6]

This conclusion is actually fortified by the legends which have for many centuries clung to the spot. Here, it was said, came Moses on his flight from Egypt, arriving without food and with feet lacerated by a rapid nine days' march. Here were, at one time, actually exhibited the well and the stone which he lifted from it to water the flocks of Shuweib (Jethro). Here, too, was shown a rock from which the water gushed out at his command.[7] All this is very well, but, in fact, an earlier version of the last legend placed this same rock at Petra! It would surely be wiser to regard

[1] Gen. x. 7; Hab. iii. 7; cf. Musil, *N.H.*, p. 287.   [2] Job vi. 19.
[3] Musil, *N.H.*, p. 293.   [4] Ibid. p. 289.
[5] Ib., pp. 278 ff., Appendix IX.
[6] Hence Musil locates Horeb by the Sheib (Wadi) of el-Hrob between Beda and el-Hraibe (p. 263), though there is, apparently, no mountain of this name.   [7] Musil, *N.H.*, pp. 279–81.

such Arab folklore as devoid of any further foundation than might have been provided by Christian or Jewish piety in the later centuries of the Roman Empire. *Non tali auxilio!* The existence of this 'city of Madian' on the east coast of the Gulf of Akaba is important only as a general indication of the regions once ruled by Midian; it cannot be accepted as trustworthy evidence for the territories which this people occupied in its prime. For this we must have recourse to the earliest Biblical traditions; and these, while they locate the Midianites with equal clearness to the east of the rift of the Arabah, reveal at the same time how much wider was the sphere of their influence. Their connexion with the oases of Tema and Dedan and with the important trading centres of the Yemen and African Cush is not the only proof of their ancient greatness. Equally suggestive are their relations with the marauding tribes of the interior, whose distinctive title, Bene Kedem, the Children of the East, is found side by side with that of Midian in the narrative of Judges vi–viii. It is clear from this story of their invasion of Palestine and subsequent defeat by Gideon that the Midianites were at this date sufficiently powerful to overrun the whole of Transjordania, though it is difficult to believe that they held it permanently. Their true northern boundary seems, indeed, to have lain between the land of Moab and the Wadi Sirhan. It was at Karkor[1] (Keraker) at the northern end of this Wadi that the routed hosts halted in their flight, and their mistaken sense of security suggests strongly that they had by this time regained their own borders. Certainly at the time of Israel's approach to Moab their encampments were to be found in the neighbourhood of that country, since their elders were consulted, and employed as ambassadors, by Balak.[2] We shall probably be not far from the truth if we accept this line as marking, normally, the northward limit of their expansion. For their southern boundary the evidence is less precise but it may be taken as

---

[1] Judges viii. 10; Musil, *N.H.*, p. 284.   [2] Num. xxii. 4, 7.

including, at the least, the oasis of Dedan (el-'Ala);[1] while, to the east, the great desert of el-Nefud would form a natural barrier. When we turn to the west the answer is not so simple. It would be easy to suppose, from a casual study of the map, that the boundary of Midian on this flank would be limited only by the coast. There are, however, strong objections to this view. The physical features of the country are definitely against it;[2] and there is one small but possibly important clue in the account of Moses' wanderings as a shepherd which points unmistakably in the same direction. On taking charge of the flock of his father-in-law, he is said to have led it 'to the back' (i.e. to west) of the pasture-land of Midian.[3] Now this expression is meaningless if the pastures lay along the coasts of the Gulf of Akaba or the Red Sea; but it is readily intelligible if the normal grazing-lands of Midian lay on the lofty Arabian plateau, east of the coastal range. To the *west* of this plateau there stretches the inhospitable tract of el-Hismeh, continued southwards in the still wilder lava-fields (Harras) of el-Raha and el-Awaridh; while the chain of granite mountains which separates them from the maritime lowlands of el-Tihamah forms a natural 'edge' or 'lip' to the whole of this portion of the Northern Hejaz.[4] It is here then rather than along the coast that we should naturally place the western boundary of Midian.

2. *The Topography.* The territory thus defined extends far beyond the limits of the present survey and it will be necessary to focus attention only upon the parts of it which link the Harras with the head of the Gulf of Akaba. A word must be said, however, on a second and much smaller volcanic tract which might seem at first sight to be more appropriate for the site of Horeb. This tract lies upon the eastern borders of Mount Seir (Jebel el-Shera), about 15 miles north of Ma'an, and its position suggests that it may

---

[1] See above, p. 202.   [2] See below, § 2.   [3] Exod. iii. 1.
[4] This range is still called el-Shefa, the 'lip' or 'brink' of the eastern highlands.

have been directly responsible for the overthrow of the Cities of the Plain. It is, however, precisely this position which would seem to disqualify it from having any connexion with the 'Mount of God'. It is true that the Song of Deborah (followed later by the 'Blessing of Moses' and the prophet Habakkuk) seems to favour the association with Mount Seir and the 'field of Edom',[1] but this evidence is counterbalanced by statements which clearly contradict it. A curious note at the beginning of Deuteronomy[2] gives the distance from Horeb to Kadesh-barnea (the High Place of Petra) as eleven days' march 'by the way of Mount Seir', an estimate which can have no meaning if the Mount was merely situated on the eastern border of Edom. It is, in fact, clear both from this statement and from the traditional forty days' journey of Elijah that Horeb was conceived as lying at some hundreds of miles' distance from Palestine, and it is difficult to understand how such a belief could have arisen if it was actually in a district so near, and so well known, to Israel. Where the evidence is so indecisive a definite conclusion is obviously impossible, but it will be assumed in what follows that it is the southern lava-fields which possess the true site of Horeb, even if the actual mountain itself has not been discovered by Dr. Musil.[3]

(i) *El-Jeles and el-Tihamah.* To the traveller advancing eastward from the head of the Gulf of Akaba (the 'Yam Suph' of Solomonic days and of the Exodus Tradition)[4] the mountain range which forms the eastern edge of the Arabah seems to present an impenetrable barrier. This range, behind which the great massif of Mount Seir rises to the north-east, sweeps past the head of the gulf which it follows closely as far as the oasis of Hakl. From this point it bends

---

[1] Judges v. 4–5; Deut. xxxiii. 2; Hab. iii. 3 (where Teman is a district of Edom not to be confused with the oasis of Tema).

[2] Deut. i. 1.   [3] See above, p. 152.

[4] 1 Kings ix. 26; Exod. xiii. 18; Num. xxi. 4. (See Sayce, *Higher Criticism and the Monuments*, 1894, p. 255 f.)

away to the south-east, and though it throws off outliers towards the oases of el-Hraibe and Sharma, its general trend is henceforth in the same direction. Hence it is that the coastal strip, which, as far as Hakl, has narrowed almost to a thread, widens out into a maritime lowland, called (for this reason) el-Tihamah.[1] The mountain range itself is known by various names, the commonest to-day being el-Jeles, the 'rocky plain'. On some maps it appears as Jebel el-Shefa, the 'lip' or 'brink' of the lofty uplands of the Nejd.[2] A third name, Jebel el-Tihamah, though sometimes used, is misleading and should be avoided, since it is to the plateau above and not to the maritime plains below that these mountains most truly belong. At a point somewhat to the north-east of the oasis of Sharab in the Tihamah, this continuous range breaks up into groups of separate mountains diverging gradually towards the south-west;[3] and on the uplands behind there is a corresponding gap between the two lava-fields, Harrat el-Raha and Harrat el-Awaridh. A line drawn roughly through these points to the Hejaz railway forms the southern boundary of the important tribe, the Beni 'Atiyyeh,[4] the entire range of el-Jeles northward to Mount Seir forming their western border. These boundaries are worthy of special notice because they show how readily the tribal territories of the Hejaz conform with the marked physical divisions of the country. Though not co-extensive with those of ancient Midian in its prime, the present territories of the Beni 'Atiyyeh must, to a large extent, be the same. It is, in fact, the tribe which holds the uplands and controls the main caravan routes from Medina to Damascus which enjoys also the longest sweep of territory and the widest horizons. In the Tihamah, by way of contrast, the corresponding stretch of country is divided in

---

[1] From Taham a 'low unhealthy maritime region', Burton, *Gold Mines of Midian*, p. 125 n.

[2] Burton, loc. cit.   [3] Musil, *N.H.*, p. 132.

[4] Ib., p. 236. (This was at least true in 1910.)

its southern portion between the two tribes of the Beli and the Huweytat el-Tihamah (an offshoot of the Huweytat tribe which borders on Mount Seir), while beyond el-Hraibe the clans of Imran and el-Mesaid hold between them the mountains and the shore. It is noticeably in this, the northernmost and narrowest section of el-Tihamah (that which contains Beda, the 'City of Madian'), that the tribal boundaries are least clearly delimited. Although one of the old pilgrim routes to Medina passes through it from Akaba to Sharma, it is, in effect, a backwater, whose inhabitants isolated into minor groups maintain little contact with the main stream of Hejazi life. It may, indeed, be safely asserted that whatever fate drove a remnant of the tribe of Midian into this corner, it is neither here nor anywhere in the lowlands of el-Tihamah that we must seek their ancient boundaries. It is, of course, possible that it was this lower route through Hakl, Sharma, and Sharab which Moses followed in his first journey to Midian, though its defiles and confined spaces must be ill suited to the passage of a large body of persons with flocks and herds; but as it is the uplands, with their lava-fields, which concern us, we may leave the maritime regions and return to our starting-point at Akaba and the mountain barrier which overhangs it. To penetrate this obstacle by direct approach is impossible; it is necessary to proceed more than an hour's ride to the north, and then swing eastward into the black gorge of the Wadi el-Ithm, the main, and in this region the only, pass from the rift of el-Araba to the highlands of the Hejaz. At the summit of its tortuous and airless course, this ravine breaks out from the mountains into a level plain; and the road which has followed it forks at this point in two directions. Northward the trade route to Ma'an climbs steadily the ascent to Mount Seir, which it penetrates by the pass of Shtar. Eastward the old pilgrim el-Hismeh road bends sharply away across an expanse of sandy hills and the remarkable uplands of el-Hismeh.

(ii) *El-Hismeh.* This extraordinary tract demands a more detailed description. 'It is a white rocky plain, eroded by rain, wind, and sand, upon which are found the numberless scattered, brown remains of various firmer strata.'[1] On the north-east this plain is bordered by the el-Shera range (Mount Seir) and on the west by that of el-Jeles. To the south there stretches an uninterrupted expanse, over 120 miles long, of scoured and wind-swept upland; while on the east a series of sandy plains and depressions closes at an average breadth of 50 miles the other flank of this fantastic and forbidding wilderness. Viewed from the outlying slopes of Mount Seir, an astonishing panorama is presented; 'above the dense haze there rose like islets countless horns, cones and truncated cones, pyramids, obelisks, and other quaint shapes, fashioned by the action of rain, frost, and wind, which had gnawed at the layers of rock and carried away the softer ingredients to the east and south-east as far as the sandy desert el-Nefud. The rays of the rising sun were reflected from the separate peaks in a dense shower of golden sparks, while the sides turned away from the sun were wrapped in a dark red shadow.'[2] Such is the aesthetic aspect of el-Hismeh, but it is significant that on the international map of these regions it still remains a featureless blank. No road passes down its long expanse; for the pilgrim route which enters at its north-west corner hurries across it eastward to the easier avenue now occupied by the Hejaz railway. In all the length and breadth of it there is no sign of an oasis. Sweltering under the glare of a blazing sun, scarred and riven by the icy fingers of winter, swept by pitiless blinding sandstorms,[3] its crazy hills bear witness to the penalty which they have paid to the forces of Nature. Truly for those who knew the green flats of the Delta or the smooth outlines of the Palestinian hills or even the rolling

[1] Musil, *N.H.*, p. 48.
[2] Ib., p. 34.
[3] Ib., p. 159. (The explorer was himself caught in one of these storms.)

downlands of the Negeb, the memory of such a place must have retained the horror of a nightmare. Is there not here at least a part of that 'terrible wilderness' which once lay between Israel and the Promised Land?

(iii) *The Harras.* So far we have not dealt with the southern boundary of this waste. 'A black rampart, as if heaped up by giants'[1] rises beyond, and closes it in on this side. This is the lava-field of Harrat el-Raha, which extends some 80 miles to the south-east, and is resumed after an interval as the Harrat el-Awaridh. For the most part the Harra is 'an endless plain covered with black lava',[2] and with only the slightest traces of vegetation. Tracks, where they occur, wind in and out among gloomy crags, over sharp lava stones, through narrow rocky defiles. One short passage of description from the explorer's actual experience will suffice to reveal the character of this dreadful desolation. 'The river bed was gray, the rocky walls white below, black above, and overhead hovered an ash-coloured veil of air which blazed with the glowing heat. I trembled with ague, Rif'at complained that he had a severe headache, Tuman's eyes were inflamed, red, and swollen, the guide . . . asked for his wages, and announced that he would leave us immediately; two of the camels had their backs lacerated and bleeding, their feet were already terribly torn by the stones; all were tired and hungry, and we had to press on.'[3] Yet appalling as were the hardships of this section of the journey, the view from the summit of the lava-plateau must have been at least a partial reward. 'To the west we could see on the Sinai Peninsula not only the mountains of the southern part of the peninsula, but also the plain extending to the north of these mountains. Nearer to us towered the steep peaks of Harb and Debbar, and to the south we had a view of the greater part of the at-Tihama shore. We were travelling at a height of about 1,460 metres (4,788 feet).

[1] Musil, *N.H.*, p. 156.
[2] Ib., p. 190.
[3] Musil, loc. cit.

Around us extended a black, lifeless, slightly undulating plain that stretched beyond the limits of our vision. The deep narrow ravines seemed to be blacker than the plain itself.' Two points may be noticed in this description, before we pass on. The *direct range* of view to the plains of the Sinai Peninsula from this corner of the Harra is at the least 160 miles. This will give some idea of the conditions of visibility which obtain around these coasts, and make it easy to understand how a colossal pillar of smoke, belched forth from these lofty uplands, could be seen by watchers hundreds of miles away.[1] The reference to Jebel Harb is also of interest, because the resemblance of its name to Horeb has inclined some scholars to identify it with the Mount of God.[2] Harb, however, like its sister mountain, Debbar, is not a volcano, but an isolated peak in the black granite range of el-Jeles. For the true site of Horeb we must search within the Harras themselves, where scores of extinct volcano cones rear their heads from the wilderness of the craggy plateau around. It is, indeed, on the fringe of the Harrat el-Raha where it fades away with the disappearance of its mountain-brink upon the west that we find, quite unexpectedly, the place we seek.

(iv) *El-Gaa and Tadra*. The interval between the two Harras of el-Raha and el-Awaridh is filled by the green basin of the hospitable plain, el-Gaa. The approach to this plain from the west is by way of the Wadi Abu Hamata, a broad defile 'enclosed by high sandstone rocks covered with a stratum of lava', and a similar pass carries the road through the Harrat el-Awaridh to the more open avenue occupied by the Hejaz railway. As the traveller advances eastward through the Wadi Abu Hamata, he finds the valley broadening out into a basin enclosed on all sides by low, but steep, slopes. This is el-Gaa, the 'watering-place', as it is significantly called, from the unusually large number of rain-water

[1] The actual distance to Suez is about 400 miles, but see p. 142.
[2] McNeile, p. cv.

tanks with which it has been provided by Nature. Its surface is 'covered with a fairly deep layer of clay, in which various plants thrive luxuriously, and it therefore forms the best winter encampment of the Beli. The guide proudly pointed out to us the abundant withered pasturage through which we were passing, and asked whether throughout our journey from Tebuk we had seen so many and such various plants. The annuals were yellowish, while the shrubs were a brilliant green.'[1] Penetrating still further eastward into this plain, the track crosses, on the left, the course of a broad valley, the Wadi Dherwa, which, running from north to south, divides the table mountains on the west of el-Gaa from the similar, but isolated mountain of Tadra to the east. Another valley, the Wadi el-Nejileh, coming also from the north, not only joins the Wadi Dherwa on this side, but completes the isolation of Tadra on its eastern flank as well. High up this second valley, under the northern slopes of the mountain, are situated the wells Kulban Htzer, and near these is reported to be a holy place, el-Manhal, upon which there are twelve stones, known as el-Madhbah (the Place of Sacrifice). The Beli tribesmen are reported to be still in the habit of offering sacrifices on this altar when they are encamped in the plain. In the Wadi Dherwa, on the western slopes of Tadra, there is said to have been at one time a spring, now clogged up by a collapse of rock. South-west of Tadra the plain is overlooked by the hill of Tor Hamde, to which a further reference will be made below. To the south-east is the volcano of el-Azi, in which are 'the caves of the servants of Moses' (Moghayer 'Abid Musa), where the prophet's retinue is said to have sheltered while their master was abiding with Allah. It is unwise, as we have already seen, to rely too far on these Arab folk-tales, but the reader will have already noticed several details curiously reminiscent of Exodus. We come now to the mountain itself. So

---

[1] Musil, *N.H.*, p. 214. The account which follows is derived almost verbatim from the explorer's narrative.

far we have called it Tadra, but this name only refers to the lower part of it. This is described by the explorer as a grey table-mountain (presumably of some lime- or sand-stone), upon the eastern slopes of which rises a black volcanic cone, bearing the name Hala el-Bedr.[1] This volcano, we are told, is regarded by the surrounding Bedouin as a holy mountain, and this seems to be amply confirmed by the existence at its foot of the sacred spot el-Manhal 'where various signs and inscriptions are said to be carved on sacrificial boulders'.[2] 'Tadra and the entire surrounding district is associated with various legends. The volcano of el-Bedr is said once to have vomited fire and stones, destroying many Bedouins and their camels and sheep. Since then the Bedouins have been afraid to ascend this volcano and they drive away their animals, not allowing them to graze upon the slopes or upon the grey ridge of Tadra.' There is a legend connected with this volcano which sounds curiously like a confused version of Elijah's sojourn at the Brook Cherith, which, since the prophet visited the Mount of God, may not be altogether without relevance. Beneath el-Bedr 'there was once encamped a Bedouin 'belonging to the men of vision' (ahl as-sirr)—i.e. acquainted with what is a secret to others. This Bedouin had intercourse with heavenly spirits. When his tribe wished to migrate and to seek better territory for their flocks, he dissuaded them. . . . But his fellow tribesmen would not listen to him. They departed, and the man of vision was left deserted with his daughter Hamda near the volcano of el-Bedr. He used to sit in the summit of the volcano and his daughter upon its spur, which was named Tor Hamde after her. Every day Allah sent them an eagle, which gave half-a-loaf to the man of vision and half-a-loaf to his daughter.'[3] This continued for twenty years, when

---

[1] Musil shows on his map another cone also called Hala Bedr some miles to the east.

[2] Musil, *N.H.*, p. 216.

[3] Ib., p. 215.

MEDITERRANEAN SEA

UMM EL AKAREB
DEAD SEA

THE NEGEB

PELUSIUM The Way of the Land of the Philistines

TANIS
(ZOAN)

AIN KADEIS

Volcanic field

FENÁN
EN NAHAS
PETRA MAAN

EGYPT

SUEZ

The Way of the Wilderness of the Yam Suph

NEKHL

EL MENIYYEH

AKABA

PENINSULA
OF
SINAI

HAKL

GULF OF SUEZ

Jebel el Shefa or el Jeles

BEDA

Jebel Musa

TEBUK

TOR

EL HRAIBE
SHARMA
RWAFA

EL MUWEILIH

■ TOWNS
◉ SITES

RED SEA

SHARAB

TADRA
HALA EL BEDR

BADA

To TEIMA
60 miles

To EL ALA
60 miles

EL ARABA

GULF OF AKABA (YAM SUPH)

HISMEH

HEJAZ RAILWAY

THE LAND OF MIDIAN

TIHAMAH

ECYPT & MIDIAN

10 0 10 20 30 40 50 60
ENGLISH MILES

the remnants of the tribe returned after many failures and, thereafter following the holy man's advice, enjoyed once more their lost prosperity. It is, of course, quite possible that both this and the legend of the 'servants of Moses' have found their way through Christian and Jewish channels into these regions; but if this is so, it is at least strange that there is no suggestion of a legend identifying this holy volcano with the Mount of God.

GENERAL INDEX

Aaron, 66, 74, 120
his prominence a sign of late redaction, 51, 87; an essential element of the Tradition, 63; change of attitude toward, 71, 87; claimed as Levite, 100; his connexion with Golden-Calf-story, 109, 110–11, 115; nature of his sin, 111, 113; his death, 111

Abarim, mountain of, 67

Abiathar, survives massacre at Nob, 86, 97, 115; priest of Ark in Jerusalem, 98, 99; supports Adonijah and is banished, 102; his fall permits growth of Levitical power, 102

Abimelech of Gerar, 44

Abinadab, guardian of Ark, 88

Abishai's defeat of Edom, 192

Abraham, 43; at Hebron, 44; his predominance over Isaac, 46

Absalom, 75, 81

Achan, 97

Achor, Valley of, 29

Aden, 166

Adonijah, 102

Aetiology, defined, 62; its presence in O.T., 62–3; types of, 63; examples of, 65–77; signs of, 68; importance of the method, 78; cumulative weight of evidence, 122

Ahaz, 193

Ahijah, *see* Ahimelech

Ahimelech, priest of Nob, 96, 97, 98

Ahitub, Ichabod's brother, 86, 94

Aila, 202

Akaba (town), 202, 207

Akaba, Gulf of, 123, 124, 142, 157, 202, 204
not Sea divided before Israel, 168–9; 'Yam Suph', 205

Akrabbim, Ascent of, still known by same name, 194, 195

el-Ala, Dedan, 202, 204

Amalek, 126

Amalekites, 96, 97, 189, 190, 201

Amaziah, captures Sela-Petra, 193

Amenhotep II, 47; Pharaoh of the Exodus, 52 n.

Amon Re, deity of imperial Egypt, 49

Amos, his message to Israel, 24, 25, 30; his dislike of luxury, 26–7

Analysis, textual, critical, its achievements, 58, 60, 67, 119; subordinate to knowledge of psychology and history, 60; its limitations, 67, 68

Anathoth, 102

Andes, volcanic eruptions in, 165

Aphek, results of Philistine victory at, 91; cause of disaster, 113, 115

Arabah, 126, 155, 157, 169, 201; Israelite occupation of, 69, 127, 133, 187ff.; possible base of reconnaissance, 128; mineral resources, 189; Israel's struggles for, 189, 192; Kadesh-barnea in, 196

Arabia Petraea, 201

Ararat, 44

Ark of God, the, 33, 35, 41, 45, 63, 115, 117, 119, 127, 150
Divine Palladium of Israel, 80, 117, 134; carried before the army, 81, 87; its recovery David's masterstroke, 81, 82; symbol of Israel's unity, 82; starting-point for investigation of Tradition, 83; its contents, and theories regarding, 84 and note, 85, 106; revered for sake of contents 85, for itself 108; capture and return

PASSAGES OF SCRIPTURE QUOTED